TROUBLED WATERS

Cover Designed by Jennifer Telfer
Edited by Bradley Angle

This book is a work of nonfiction. Names, Rates and Ranks are often removed or abbreviated to protect individuals.

by Laurie Powell

Stay engaged at:
https://www.facebook.com/groups/thelegacyofobie
https://twitter.com/of_obie

Printed in the United States of America

First Printing: January 2021
Amazon

ISBN
978-0-578-82191-7
978-0-578-82192-4

TROUBLED WATERS

The Legacy of USCG Hero BM3 Travis R. Obendorf ~ OBIE

By his mom
Laurie Powell

I dedicate this book, of course to my son: The Hulk, Gentle Giant, Muscle Hamster, Viking Warrior, Hero; always My Hero and now, my Beautiful Angel ~ OBIE. To his friends, shipmates and to all Veterans, those that we still have and those that we have lost. All Active Military, as well as all Law Enforcement, Firefighters, First Responders, etc. All of these people sacrifice for us daily. They put their lives on the line, they get paid the least and they do the most! They suffer from the after effects of what they have seen and experienced (PTSD) and are denied the recognition and help that is SO deserved. They are even afraid to go and seek the help they need for fear of repercussions from their superiors and the stigma that has been instilled throughout society. We lose an average of 22 Veterans a day due to suicide because of this. The Coast Guard itself has the highest ratio of suicides among the military forces. This is all a tragedy! God Bless you all!

— Laurie Powell

CONTENTS

Remembered Joy
Don't grieve for me, for now I'm free!
I follow the plan God laid for me.
I saw His face, I heard His call,
I took His hand and left it all....
I could not stay another day,
To love, to laugh, to work or play;
Tasks left undone must stay that way.
And if my parting has left a void,
Then fill it with remembered joy.
A friendship shared, a laugh, a kiss....
Ah yes, these things I, too, shall miss.
My life's been full, I've savored much:
Good times, good friends, a loved-one's touch.
Perhaps my time seemed all to brief-
Don't shorten yours with undue grief.
Be not burdened with tears of sorrow,
Enjoy the sunshine of the morrow.

—AN IRISH BLESSING

(I LOVE YOU MY SON ~ MY BEAUTIFUL ANGEL)

FOREWORD

TRAVIS' ACCIDENT AND SUBSEQUENT PASSING CRIPPLED ME with sadness and hurt. The initial weeks following his loss were particularly challenging. I noticed myself feeling guilty for not devoting time to grieve. I thought: "I haven't seen or spoken to this poor guy in over a year; what are these feelings, and what is their purpose?" His loss began to interfere with my entire life from work to home. Time passed, but the hurt did not subside.

I reached out to his family, and was especially concerned for his mother. In my letter to Laurie, I commiserated as best I could with the enormity of her pain, which I could only imagine. My love and friendship for her and her family has grown exponentially. Our "pen pal" style relationship via email continues to this day.

Laurie and I exchanged the very early workings of this book several years ago. And as I wrote about Travis, I became tearful and would think: "Why am I doing this to myself?"

When Obie and I served together, he was subordinate in rank, yet a few years older, which made for an interesting dynamic. Never difficult to supervise, his work ethic, healthy lifestyle and mentoring abilities were impeccable. Travis would volunteer to orient incoming personnel and even entertain distinguished military guests at my request. Although we could have been closer, he made a huge impact on me due to the depth of his character.

One of my fondest memories of Travis occurred on a boat in Boston Harbor. He and several crew members were discussing and strategizing how to improve the "randomized" selection of cleaning duties back at the station. The senior personnel on the boat exclaimed "rank has its privileges," leaving little room for rebuttal. Travis was clearly frustrated by the response and remarked, "Yeah, but it's the principle," suggesting that we work as a team regardless of hierarchical position.

I became interested in creative writing as a child and can remember being curious about the utility and power behind storytelling. My curiosity propelled into questioning whether or not writing about the loss of a loved one would yield therapeutic effects for the author. As it turns out, it's a mixed bag. The writing process has certainly helped me grieve his loss although it was an extremely painful process. I've always been skeptical of "curative" interventions for grief, seeing how there are no practical alternatives to non-existence.

The following story not only highlights Travis' character and humility as a Coast Guard serviceman, it demonstrates the various dangers and adverse conditions our members of the armed forces encounter on a daily basis. Although there were several variables that likely contributed to his passing, some were more avoidable than others. To his successors, "It's the principle". His loss has united Coast Guard service members and family members in a remarkable way. His loss remains visceral for those who loved him.

- Dr. Julion Marrinan, Coast Guard Veteran

INTRODUCTION

I love the CG as well, but my son did not have to die. I also know that there is light and dark in all things. There was a whole lot of dark that happened that day and the days to follow to hide and portray a totally different story. Yes, they admitted to equipment failure, they had to, it was obvious.....the rest.....
—within a letter to the editor, from Laurie Powell

AFTER MY SON PASSED, his shipmates contacted me often. Their calls were sometimes triggered by reflections, or reminders, like the sight of a passing bird. They'd tell me energized stories – memories they shared with Obie. Some told me of dreams in which Obie came to them to let them know that he was at peace and that he was always watching over them. Regularly I found myself in this situation, sometimes multiple times a month, always grateful they trusted me and were willing to reach out... Listening through an impersonal plastic phone, muting the sounds of my tears, I'd think proudly, that these callers surely reflected the web of friendships Obie made during his 9 years in the United States Coast Guard.

Often these conversations would drift to the night of the incident. The voices would recount that horrible moment, time and time again, start to finish, so detailed; and then they would stop, always, in cold phone static silence. The callers would say "I'm so sorry." And I'd plead with them that it was ok. "It's alright. I understand. You were a good friend to my son. It was tragic and traumatic for all of us." You have suffered as well, and these are things I need to know.

These calls were not only memories, reflections, apologies and tears. So many people loved my son. Collectively, I began to see another element these calls represented. Grief is a turbulent process, not only for me... I am so very thankful for those voices.

The pages that follow contain the legacy that my son BM3 Travis R. Obendorf left in his wake for the United States Coast Guard. Known by so many personalized nicknames - Obie, Trav, Hulk, Viking Warrior, The Muscle Hamster - he was in his 9th year of service when he lost his life. Included, to the best of my ability, are the tragic circumstances of his death. In my search for answers, it's true I became angry, though that's not what Obie would have wanted. My anger has faded. Now, I'm left with immense sadness and emptiness. Within these pages are years of my research, and a collection of testimonies from his friends and shipmates. The troubled waters are still there if one looks. My conclusion is simple, though I'm leaving the material necessary for you to draw your own.

My son did not have to die.

I greatly respect the Coast Guard for what they do and represent. I am so proud of Trav, for everything he did while serving. So proud of all the men and women - the guts of the Coast Guard – for what they do, what they sacrifice, and what they represent. The politics of the senior command is where I stop my appreciation. The circumstances of my son's tragedy and the "investigation" that followed, shows they've lost track of what is most important - their people. The Coast Guard's publicized framework was: "HE DIED SO OTHERS MAY LIVE." My conclusion: this was not an accident, it was preventable; self-interest and complacency were behind my son's death! I will never forgive the command for putting the lives of their crew in such low regard and then passing the blame to them.

Through my grieving process, I will eventually move onwards with the knowledge that a lesson will be learned here. My son will not die in vain. His death will not be veiled behind a curtain of pomp. The crew of his ship, the Waesche, will know they are not to blame. His legacy will live, and those who know it will grow as individuals and as leaders.

This book is to that end. It is to the legacy of my son, the truth of the events and decisions that took his life, and the tragedy that followed his injuries. It is a description of the Coast Guard's TROUBLED WATERS. It is THE LEGACY OF USCG HERO BM3 TRAVIS R. OBENDORF ~ OBIE.

PART 1

Travis Raymond Obendorf
April 6th, 1985 – December 18, 2013

OBIE'S EARLY LIFE

It was as if he had the Happy Flu.
—Friend and Shipmate

OST PARENTS ARE PROUD OF THEIR CHILDREN and all parents would like to be. It's not unusual for parents to go overboard in praising them, and I am no exception. I am grateful for every moment of every day I had with my son. He arrived as God's gift to us on April 6th, 1985. To me, and others, he was a beautiful soul and a hero every day of his too-short, twenty-eight-year life.

Even his entrance into this world was a glimpse as to the type of person and strong will that he brought with him. We had a hard time getting him aboard! After eighteen hours of labor we got it done and he arrived, weighing 7 pounds 9 ounces and was 21 ½ inches long. He was a little marked up and bruised, but he was beautiful! We were all surprised at his length. He definitely didn't get his height from either of his parents. He took after his great-grandfather in stature.

Holding him for the first time, and gazing down at him, I looked into the most amazing blue-grey eyes. His blonde hair would turn into the most beautiful curly locks. But his first days, like his whole life, were an adventure.

Two crises happened the first day after bringing him home. His air passages had not been properly cleaned out. We managed to open them up the first time, but the second time, while I was so intent on changing his diaper, I suddenly realized that he'd become so still—too still. I looked into his face and saw that he was blue! Sweeping him up in my arms, I ran into the dining room and called the paramedics. By the time they arrived he was breathing again, and later that day he expelled a large mass that had been restricting his air passage. That was no easy beginning for a new baby and it absolutely scared the hell out of his new parents!

Even so, Trav, as he grew from stage to stage, was a wonderful child and remained a wonderful child. Of course, he made mistakes, we had rough patches - I'm not saying he was perfect. Who is, after all! As a family we sometimes struggled, but through everything he really was a great kid. He experienced the usual growing pains as he tested the waters of life. In his younger years, we spent countless hours constructing creations with Legos. He loved Legos. He played with his numerous Teenage Mutant Ninja Turtles, Leonardo being his favorite.

Halloween was a fun holiday for us. We held annual Pumpkin Carves with family and friends. Everyone would carve pumpkins and then we'd have a contest, great food, and a lot of laughs. Obie was quite good as an artist as well. He ran track and played soccer. He rode motorcycles and loved music, almost all music, even classical, though he wasn't much of a fan of old-time Country. He played football and basketball and absolutely loved video games and martial arts. He was fond of Robin Hood stories, Braveheart and Gladiator, and anything to do with the Renaissance, Celts, and Vikings and bagpipes. Family and friends, of course, were very important to him as well.

Obie was a very kind, caring and generous person. He was always present and there for you, even if he didn't know you. He couldn't stand bullies or bullying, and though he wasn't by nature a fighter, mistreat someone and you'd be answering to him. Though gentle at heart, he still cultivated a love of martial arts and boxing. In fact, he had talked of training in kick-boxing. Obie was a true friend. He'd do anything for anyone, even giving you the shirt off his back and the last dollar in his wallet if he thought you needed them and he had been known to do just that.

Obie's personality grew with age just like his stature – to 6' and 225lbs! He gave the most amazing hugs, great big Bear Hugs, and his laugh would fill a room. It was infectious. No one could remain sad or in a bad mood for long with Obie nearby. He had the most radiant smile that came straight from his heart and his heart was just about as big as they come. Obie's goal was to make people happy and to see them smile. He was one of those rare people who always made efforts to ease others' pain. This was what he wanted people to know of him outwardly. He kept his inner struggles to himself.

I don't mean to suggest that he was deeply serious all the time - far from it. Obie was a prankster with a great sense of humor. He loved joking around. We noticed this trait when he was very young. He loved to hide and jump out to scare me even when he was little. His laugh saved him from any reprimand, because honestly, the moment he started laughing you just couldn't be mad at him. He got such a kick out of it. Soon, you were laughing, too. He was such a gift...

Obie's father and I divorced when he was quite young and it devastated him. It was bumpy for a time. We went through new relationships and marriages that proved not to be the best. It's true that when you have a child, he or she sometimes suffers the consequences of choices made by the parents. Someone once said that adults can choose, while a child can't. There's more than a little painful truth in that phrase. In time, both his father and I found partners and entered into successful marriages in which Obie was loved by our spouses as if he had been their own.

* * *

S O, HOW DOES A YOUNG MAN FROM IDAHO wind up in the Coast Guard, and why our son in particular?

Just about all Americans were devastated by 9/11 and Trav seemed especially affected. He was sixteen at the time and wanted to help in any way he could, but was too young just yet. That's the kind of young man he was. He had a desire to contribute combined with an ongoing inner debate about his future plans. What did he want to do?

Obie had thought a lot about college, but the truth was he didn't love school. I understood that. We aren't all scholars or particularly well suited to college life. I've always believed that there are "book" people and "life-experience" people. Some people are both. My son was a life-experience person. I identified with him because I'm the same way.

His father, though, very much believed in going to college. He went to college and even worked as a school teacher at one time. He couldn't understand his son's reluctance to continue his education after high school and he was disappointed. So, his father's solution was for him to join the military. His dad presented this to Obie as a win-win opportunity. Obie's need to contribute in terms of helping others would be met and he would continue to learn valuable skills while on the job; and he could possibly go on to an education after serving. This really wasn't a bad idea. It all sounded great to Trav. And after making up his mind, he presented me with the idea in the same way his father presented it to him.

I'll never forget the day he told me he was signing up for the Coast Guard, or the phrase that left me resigned in subtle but accepting discontent... I'll be honest - I fell apart. It was a true mom moment. I melted down thinking of my son traveling to who knew where and finding himself continually in harm's way. I'm sure the recruiters painted a rosy picture of Coast Guard life. All recruiters do, it's their job. But the words he said to me that day echo through my mind constantly and always will. "Mom," Obie said, "IT'S THE COAST GUARD. NOTHING BAD IS GOING TO HAPPEN TO ME."

If only that had been true! Most people have no idea about the real, everyday life in the Coast Guard. If they did, they'd have much more respect for those who serve.

* * *

Obie took the Oath of Enlistment, swearing to obey the orders of the officers appointed over him. That was his final step to becoming committed to attend Basic Training at USCG Training Center Cape May shortly after high school. Just before he had to go, his stepdad Chad and I gave him a graduation trip of his choice, anywhere he wanted to go. Obie decided that he wanted to tour the lighthouses along the beautiful coast of Oregon.

The memories from that trip are wonderful in so many ways, and I will always be grateful for the time we were able to spend with him. He so enjoyed touring the lighthouses and just being near the ocean. I imagine he was thinking about how his life was going to change and wondering what a life at sea was going to be like. A totally new life for a young man from Idaho. This was the mark of my son becoming a Coast Guardsman, his deep reflection with the sea.

He graduated Basic Training on December 17th, 2004 in Cape May, New Jersey and we attended. As I watched him throughout the ceremony, bursting with pride, I couldn't help but replay the words he said to me months earlier: "Mom it's the Coast Guard. Nothing bad is going to happen to me."

What a powerful effect words can have.

BM3 OBENDORF

As days, weeks, months and years went by we continued to share the best and worst times together. All of us in the duty section had a soft spot for the "Muscle Hamster" as we referred to him. I couldn't be more proud to have known and served with him.
—USCG Shipmate, Boston

OBIE WAS SO EXCITED when he learned that he would be stationed in Astoria, aboard the Coast Guard Cutter Alert, a 210-foot medium endurance cutter. He served there from January 2005 until June 2008.

Though he was stationed in Oregon, which is not that far from Idaho, Chad and I didn't get to see him often, but we had more opportunities than if he'd been stationed almost anywhere else. Due to constant underway deployments, it was hard for us to schedule a visit, though we did so as often as we could. Every visit was wonderful. We'd rent a condo in Seaside and Obie would stay with us. This gave him a little bit of normalcy from his Coast Guard life, and we got to spend as much time with him as possible.

It was while Obie was stationed in Oregon that he began a trend I quickly grew to love. On late nights when he would pull a watch at the station, he would call me, half whispering, at two, three or four in the morning and say "Mom, I'm bored. Please talk to me. I need you to help me stay awake." It was during those early morning, after-midnight hours that he would share with me the favorite music and songs he'd discovered since the last time we'd talked and we'd just chit-chat. It's true he wasn't supposed to be doing this. In fact, he would have found himself in Deep Shit if he had been caught, but those talks remain among some of my most cherished memories. Even after he posted to other stations, we kept up what had become a tradition. The time of day that he called never mattered to me. All I knew was this: it was wonderful to be there for him and talk to him.

Like many military families with sons or daughters in the service, leave seemed to be few and far between. When Obie was able to come home, he always wanted his favorite dinner—shrimp teriyaki with Chad's famous flank steak and my breakfast bagels. Hanging around the house together, we engaged in nonstop competitions of Monopoly, Rummy and Yahtzee. Obie had been crowned "*THE MONOPOLY KING*" at a young age because he always won, and I mean always! He was truly competitive and considered it his mission to kick my butt in Rummy, he couldn't stand it that I almost always won. It was hysterical to watch how upset he'd get when he was losing, but despite his defeats we would end up in uncontrollable laughter that would leave us in tears. We laughed and laughed and laughed. They say laughter is a healer and good medicine and I know it was for us. I still have Yahtzee score cards with his name and scores on them—treasured memories. Obie also enjoyed golf with his dad, hanging out at his restaurant, playing pool, his gaming, of course, and the beauty of Idaho. And he was never without his music, he loved his music, always his music. Of course, he also exercised the luxuries of staying up late, sleeping in and leaving absolutely anything he could get away with lying around. His room would be a disaster, clothes everywhere. What I would give to be able to pick up after him again and do his laundry, or cook him another meal.

After his tour of duty in Oregon, Obie signed on to go to Bahrain – that is, he volunteered to go to the Persian Gulf. The Coast Guard name is PATFORSWA, USCG Patrol Forces Southwest Asia. It's the Coast Guard's largest unit outside of the United States. The thought of my son living and working halfway around the world was a little gut-wrenching, yet I was so proud of him. Receiving a posting to Bahrain wasn't just a matter of volunteering, he had to submit his name into a pool of applicants, then meet a host of stringent qualifications. He trained hard and met all challenges with flying colors. In fact, he achieved some of the highest scores in marksmanship. He was my rock star! Obie completed a full one-year tour in Bahrain.

While there he spent his days boarding suspicious vessels throughout the Persian Gulf. He protected the maritime port in Iraq too. Something bad happened over there, but he never wanted to talk about it. It was a difficult year for him, given some of the experience's, the culture shock, the heat and the huge distance from home.

It's also true that the experience Obie gained in Bahrain made it more difficult for him to make rate stateside. The tradeoff was not beneficial to striking Boatswain Mate, which was a hard blow to Obie, who was already dedicated and excited to earn his rating, and take on all the responsibility that came with that.

After his year in Bahrain, Obie was stationed in Boston, where he served from August 2009 until June 2013. Boston was still a long way from home, but it was a hell of a lot closer than Bahrain and it was back in the U.S.! That being said, the distance was still great enough that he was not able to come home very often, nor was it easy for us to visit him. In fact, I was only able to visit him once during his Boston tour, and this haunts me. I made the trek to celebrate his 25th birthday with him. Little did I know it would be the last birthday that I would get to celebrate with him.

The Boston Marathon Bombing occurred while he was stationed there, another tragic, senseless and impactful incident that he experienced along with the rest of the world. There is a picture of him that someone happened to capture; he was preparing one of the guns on a CG craft while getting ready to go out on patrol. You can feel the emotions and gravity of the situation by the look on his face.

Obie had made wonderful Coast Guard friends while in Boston. He had fun in many ways, and he had many great and gratifying experiences. There were some very sad experiences too (part of being in the CG), and important life lessons, but he had grown to the point where he wanted and needed something more. The significance of Obie's relationships with people can almost be measured in nicknames: *TRAV* was an obvious one he's always had. *BEAUTIFUL ANGEL* is mine. Later in the Coast Guard he was the *VIKING WARRIOR, THE GENTLE GIANT* and *THE HULK*. In Boston, some friends called him *MUSCLE HAMSTER*. And I'm sure there are so many more out there. But perhaps his proudest, even if it isn't technically a nickname, was BM3 (Boatswain mate 3rd Class), which was also the rank and rate he made when he arrived to Boston.

While there, Obie began to think about life after the Coast Guard, maybe as a chef? A wonderful cook, he would call me all the time to ask my advice or to tell me about the latest, greatest dish he'd created. He really had become an excellent cook. At one point, he asked me to look into the possibility that he might be able to attend Culinary School on the GI Bill. Unfortunately, that wasn't something that they offered. You could feel his disappointment through the phone.

Obie had been wanting to settle down for some time. He wanted a wife and a family – children and a pet. His love for animals was tremendous, though he wouldn't adopt a pet due to his hectic schedule.

He fell head over heels in love with a young woman whom I met when I visited for his birthday. I think he was seriously wanting to marry the girl, but her life path was already well established and their relationship ended. It broke his heart. In time, he met another young woman that he became quite serious about, but again, it did not work out. These heartbreaks were hard on him. When he fell for someone, he fell hard. He was such a romantic at heart, but it's hard for military members to find partners willing to have that type of life.

Because of these disappointments, Trav made up his mind to prepare for civilian life after his enlistment ended. He would get out of the Coast Guard, after 8 years of service, and start a family in Idaho. An independent life, a life he could share full-time with the people he loved.

Yet, suddenly something changed his mind about getting out. He rationalized the utility of staying in. After careful consideration, knowing that his next outfit would most likely be a larger ship, he decided that signing up for one last station made the best sense. It would put him in a better position, he reasoned, to provide for someone and a new life together.

That decision haunts me to this day and will for the rest of my life. If only he had just come home after Boston!

* * *

H IS FINAL DUTY STATION was one of the largest vessels in the Coast Guard, the 418', 112 strong crew, National Security Cutter, Waesche. Home based in Alameda, California. He was to report for duty on June 27th, 2013.

Chad and I took some comfort in the fact that at least California was closer than Boston and we thought we might get to see him more. What we didn't know is that the ship he was assigned to went out on patrol for up to four months. As a new National Security Cutter, second of the fleet, the Waesche was working hard. The upcoming patrol would be the first for the Waesche in Alaskan waters, part of Operation Artic Shield. It had to promote the new class of ships and cover for the mechanical issues taking place on her sister ships, but it also had to cover for the older class of ships, 378s, that could no longer pull their load.

Prior to reporting to Alameda, Obie was able to come home for a short visit. He left his Boston station on June 13th and drove to Idaho. Our time together was much too short. Our reunions always were.

When Obie arrived home one of the first things he did was trade in his Subaru for a badass truck. He had been talking about doing this for quite some time and finally decided the time was right. Man, did he love that truck! I have to admit, it was something to admire – a glossy white, new four-door Toyota Tacoma - and anyone that knew Obie knew that white truck of his.

We also planned for what to expect when Obie reported to the Waesche. We looked over the Welcome Aboard Package and the Ombudsman information. The Waesche was the newest ship in the fleet, equipped with the newest equipment, said its website – two helo hangers, SRP (small boats), and a stern launch. It was, I'll quote, "outfitted with the most advanced command, control, and communications equipment." The images of the ship online were exciting to Obie. Having made BM3 while in Boston, this would be the place to show his skills and advance to BM2. He pulled up photos of the SRP and told me about the way they could launch them in the middle of the ocean directly from the stern of the ship – the newest equipment and methods.

Chad and I hosted family and friends, so that people would get to see him one last time before he left for his new ship. Everyone so enjoyed seeing him, it had been years for some and the last for us all. He and I were able to have a good talk. I had the opportunity to tell him how very much I loved him and how incredibly proud I was of him, as I always had been. I'll never forget the morning that he left for Alameda. He gave me one of his big Bear Hugs, the last one that I got from him. He started to walk away and turned to flash me that big, beautiful smile with a one-handed wave, then drove away in his new truck. It would be the last time I saw my son before the incident. Full of life and ready for another new chapter.

If only he had just come home and stayed after Boston!

INCIDENT

November 11, 2013

According to a review board, faulty equipment and work practices by the crew of the cutter Waesche put Petty Officer Travis Obendorf in harm's way.
—Lauren Rosenthal, APRN – 4.24.2014

THE INCIDENT TOOK PLACE IN THE BERING SEA, near the Aleutian Islands, approximately 30 miles from the Coast Guard air station in Cold Bay. Obie had been on the Waesche for exactly four months, most of which was spent in Alaskan waters. It is the portion of Travis' legacy that ruthlessly persists in the minds of too many of his shipmates, as if it happened yesterday, over and over again. Without being there, I've had to piece together the events from multiple primary and secondary sources – but this did not spare me. After his trauma, I sat by his side for over a month, with only hope... In the beginning I heard from Obie's command that things happened one way. And through the years, I've talked to Obie's shipmates and friends that share a different story. Things never quite added up. I spent a long time researching the nature of this day, years in fact, trying to understand why those in charge made the decisions they did, before and after the incident.

To start, well, where should I start?

To start, Obie's shipmates were amazing! The crew size of the Waesche fluctuated depending on the mission but was roughly 120 men and women. On November 10, 2013, they were all working hard, at sea for months, heading to a much-needed rest at Dutch Harbor, AK. The friends my son had on that boat were so important to him and, now, to me! From the berthing area to deck-force, his shipmates and extended family, the men and women who loved him, saved his life, and prayed for his soul, the crew – they are all my heroes. And I know they each suffer in their own way.

Obie was on his first deployment with the Waesche, and though he was a seasoned Coastie, he was having a hard go of it. I know this because of the last communication I had with him before his incident. On November 7th he sent me an email describing his desire to get out of the Guard as soon as possible. As soon as they moored in Dutch Harbor, he planned to petition his command with the request. I didn't know if this was possible, but he seemed very determined. I found it unsettling as I had never heard him this upset before. Outside of his character, he told me directly in our last email communication that conditions were not good. The morale was horrible and the command was toxic. In closing our email, I told him to let me know as soon as he could how his talk went. It must be pretty bad, I thought to myself. I was very anxious to hear from him again.

I waited and checked my email often, but I didn't hear from him. Instead, the next communication I received was a phone call at 4am the morning after the incident, November 12, 2013... As we would soon learn, my son and his shipmates were set up for failure that Veterans Day. The "mission" that ended Obie's life and that changed the lives of so many of my son's shipmates was a quasi-SAR mission at best. "Quasi" because it was neither a rescue mission, nor an urgent matter. Quasi, because the subject-vessel was a part of the famous "action-packed" program - The Deadliest Catch. "Quasi" because said vessel eventually came to rest at anchor, with a sister ship, F/V Pavlof, on scene to help if needed. Quasi, because Waesche's captain had complete authority and leniency to make a decision.

We now know what the command knew then. Neither the crew nor the fishing vessel Alaska Mist were in danger. Although she lost propulsion, she was in a known location, within a reasonable anchorage, at anchor, with plenty of supplies aboard to protect both the crew and the hold of frozen fish. The crew and the ship were safe and waiting for a commercial towboat to respond.

It's true that the Waesche was ordered to the scene[1], just as they were approaching Dutch Harbor, by the District 17 Command. But it's not true that this was a "rescue."

---

[1] EMAIL 11/11/13 0711: CHIEF OF INCIDENT MANAGEMENT TO WAESCHE
"I apologize to you and your crew for diverting WAESCHE just prior to your MPB, but I need a federal response now that commercial has totally messed things up. ALASKA MIST is anchored and holding. Sister ship, F/V PAVLOF, is enroute to stand by to assist with 0930L ETA. Tug RESOLVE has one fouled screw and is standing by with intent to return to DH (Dutch Harbor) on non-folded screw. Working on identifying non-essential personnel on ALASKA MIST for possible removal by helicopters. H60 in CB (Cold Bay) is ready to respond as necessary. Intend to reposition H65 to CB (Cold Bay) for response as necessary. Need WAESCHE to assume tow if able. Will keep you posted. Thanks!"

EMAIL 0725: WAESCHE/CAPTAIN TO CHIEF OF INCIDENT MANAGEMENT
"No problem on divert - that's why we're here. We're headed enroute now and anticipate an ETA about 1600. We'll try to establish direct comms with vessel this morning to get a better understanding of their ground tackle/configuration up forward and best means to rig a tow when we arrive later today."

The Waesche was not ordered to remove the fishermen of the Alaska Mist. The Waesche was directed to report to the scene; that's it. And as they came up to speed, and sailed into the Bering Sea once more, the Waesche, the Air Crew at Cold Bay, District 17, the Central Command, and the captain of the Alaska Mist, all had their most advanced "command, control, and communications equipment" working fine – email (which I've included in in the footnotes here, and in full in Part 4). And it's apparent that the communications of The Deadliest Catch Film crew were working fine too, as we all found out.[2]

The frame the Coast Guard has defended itself with is the "but-what-if" frame. "What-if" the anchor didn't hold and the Alaska Mist drifted into the nearby basaltic cliff coast line! And that is pretty hard to argue against – as its appeal to fear is strong. But isn't there always a "what-if" in the maritime? And if that "what-if" scenario was so alarming to the Command of the Coast Guard, why not take the safer and originally suggested route and air lift the crew off? An air lift was well inside regulations. There is actually a temporary air station in Cold Bay, 30 miles from the scene, that is active every winter for this exact purpose. "What-if" the safer option was chosen, to air lift the fishermen off? Or to leave the fishermen safely at anchor until their commercial tug was repaired that afternoon? They never asked to be evacuated. Air lifts are routine for the Cold Bay air crew – and it's what happened the following day no less – once the Deadliest Catch Film Crew had enough time to get onboard. "What-if" is something I struggle with. The Search and Rescue mission was quasi at best – but more realistically, an easy excuse[3].

Looking at the big picture, all the information was there from the beginning. The Waesche could have taken less risk by not rushing in to be the hero. Instead, they planned for a specific rescue scenario hours before arriving on scene, to remove all "nonessential personnel" from the Alaska Mist. They would do this by transferring them via small boat (SRP), over three separate transfers. When they approached the anchored fishing vessel, a final safety meeting was held. And despite the new information gathered from being on scene, the Captain felt committed to the plan he communicated to Headquarters and Incident Command hours earlier. It didn't matter to him that there was new information about sea state, or that the small boat coxswain and other crew had concerns about the weather. They would do it despite the high risk

---

[2] Email 11/11/13: TO WAESCHE: PAVLOF (sister ship) is o/s standing by. 6544 should be airborne shortly enr CB with approximate one-hour flight time. RESOLVE (commercial tow) repair has been delayed until late afternoon arrival of their helo (~1700L ETA) with expected ETR later this evening. Will plan for Waesche as primary towing option with RESOLVE as back-up option.

[3] EMAIL 0920: WAESCHE/CAPTAIN TO CHIEF OF INCIDENT MANAGEMENT
"We are capable of taking them in tow. We are going to push to get there before 1600; we just came up on turbine and will run as fast as the seas/swells allow. Once onscene and wx (weather) permitting, we will put a few of our folks onboard via our small boat to assist in rigging the tow. We can remove any unnecessary personnel from the F/V at that time if desired. I'd rather do that icw taking them in tow vice later at night if condition/situation changes."

the sea-state presented – in the Red during the pre-op GAR (risk analysis) score. They would do it despite the wave height exceeding the SRP operating parameters. The command would commit to the transfer despite knowing there were multiple malfunctioning pieces of equipment on the small boat launch and retrieval platform. The Captain would give the "GO" signal despite all of these warning flags, to "rescue" the crew of the securely anchored Alaska Mist[4]. He would give the "GO" knowing that a crewmember, in this case my son, was the human-factor that had to replace the malfunctioning equipment, in the out-of-regulations sea-state, in the non-urgent situation.

But there's room to acknowledge the good too: The CO did ensure the "best coxswain" was on the SRP, but he allowed a newly qualified Ensign to have control of the bridge as OOD, to get real time experience. He mandated safety meetings all around, but then he said he would find another small boat crew when the SRP's coxswain voiced concerns. His officers had actually ignored the concerns of the small boat teams during previous missions too – always saying that they could find other crew who would do it. The CO followed his orders to report to the scene of the "SAR," but he gave the orders that lead to an unnecessary death.

And so, earlier than anticipated, the Waesche arrived on scene to find the Alaska Mist at anchor and holding[5]. Her sister ship Pavlof was in the vicinity and the nearby air station was standing by. As Obie zipped his dry suit and went through a last gear check with his fellow SRP crewmembers, he looked around to the faces of his shipmates and said "SOMEONE'S GOING TO GET HURT ON THIS ONE." And they departed for Alaska Mist.

---

[4] EMAIL 1315: INCIDENT MANAGEMENT TO WAESCHE/CAPTAIN
"Sounds great. Completely trust your judgement and will respond quickly to recommend COA. FYI, ALASKA MIST has already identified 14 non-essential personnel with eight essential personnel remaining onboard. Concur on anchor thought process. Standing by"

[5] EMAIL 1300: WAESCHE TO INCIDENT BRANCH
"Roger-we're about 30NM from ALASKA MIST position now so should be getting within VHF range soon and will brief them on our plan so they can begin to identify personnel for transfer.

WAESCHE'S STERN NOTCH DIAGRAM

*Porportions Not Scaled Equally for Ease of Comprehension
** Diagram of Properly Landed SRP with Stern Doors Closed

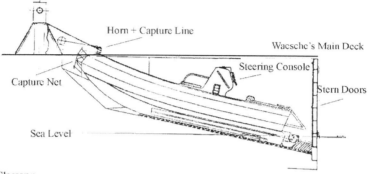

Glossary:

SRP: "Short Range Prosecutor," aka Small Boat.

Notch: The area which includes the opening for the Waesche's Small Boat

Coxswain: The captain of the small boat.

Horn: The solid post on the bow of the small boat.

Capture Line: A device to "grab" the small boat "horn," to then winch the small boat deeper into the notch.

Capture Net: A device to stableize the small boat and allow the coxswain to use additional throttle while entering the notch.

Note: The Capture Net and Harness both move further down the Ramp when the SRP is underway. When the SRP lands in the notch, it purposefully rams the capture net, at which point, if everything works properly, the Capture Line automatically grabs the SRP Horn and a winch pulls the SRP deeper into the Stern Notch. The Waesche's Capture Line never did its job, and a crew member was forced to man-handle the Capture Line into place.

T HE NOTCH DOORS WERE LEFT OPEN. Designed to protect both the notch, the small boat retrieval gear, and the small boat (SRP) itself, the Waesche's BMC wanted them shut, and he requested permission from the bridge to do so. That permission was denied. The captain thought it would be more efficient to leave the doors open, to make the passenger transfers more expedient. So, when the EO made a round to the fantail to check on the notch and the SRP landing crew he was amazed and alarmed to find the entire deck awash with raging sea water and foam.

The swells that day were reported at heights between 12 and 15 feet. The winds were reported at 20kts according to the Coast Guard Investigation, but other sources note the winds at 35knts and a meteorologist I asked to help said the winds were more likely 40 to 45kts. The sea was not orderly. The swells were coming from multiple directions, and every so often one would roll under Waesche, first lifting her stern, then smashing it into the following trough, submarining the fantail into the next wave. That is what the EO and the BMC were witnessing – Bering Sea swells smash into the Waesche's fantail and penetrate the open notch, crashing over the winches, and the capture net. They both watched with trepidation, wishing they could just shut the doors as per the Standard Operating Procedures.

At the same time, a quarter mile away, the SRP, with the crew of four, had reached the Alaska Mist. A coastie boarded the Alaska Mist to brief the fishermen, perform a basic safety inspection, and then help the fishermen don their survival suits for the passenger transfer. I was told the captain of the Alaska Mist asked why the Coast Guard was making such a big deal of everything.

Obie's small boat coxswain would only go out in such conditions if he had his most experienced and trustworthy crew. And thus, part of Obie's job was to assist the fishermen at all times. So as the first group of fishermen scrambled from the Alaska Mist to the SRP, Obie assisted, ensuring they were ready for the roller coaster they were about to experience. The SRP coxswain radioed the Waesche, saying they were enroute with the first group of passengers and they would need to re-assess the mission/weather once they returned to the ship (there were supposed to be two more transfers after that one).

An Eagle in flight could look down at the boat in the wake of the Waesche, as if it were a bathtub toy – the SRP was only 21' compared to Waesche's 418'. The SRP retrieval system is an intuitive design – a hydraulic door on the stern of the Waesche opens to a semi-submersed small boat ramp. A winch system is in place to pull the SRP up the ramp once it's locked into place. The SRP is locked in place by a "hook" on the SRP and a "capture net and line" at the top of the ramp. Simple as it sounds, it didn't work a majority of the time (only 40%). The SRP capture line would not properly latch onto the hook, leaving the SRP precariously stuck half on and half off of the Waesche. The solution was to manhandle the capture line onto the hook – which was technically against the regulations – but orders are orders, right?

Obie was located near the bow in the SRP, so he would be the one to manhandle the capture-line onto the hook once in the notch. As the SRP approached the notch, like a surfer in the zone, the coxswain matched speeds and began to count the waves. Obie transferred to the bow, and crouched into position.

The SRP moved like a spasming elevator up, then down with the swells, it was not for the faint of heart. The Waesche, however, rolled, pitched, and contorted every which way, without rhythm, against the winds and sea. The coxswain was chosen because he was the best man for the job, and true to that designation, he radioed the Waesche his intent to make final approach, and gunned the throttles. As the Waesche's stern rose like a breaching submarine, it must have been terrifying for the unaccustomed fishermen. But the coxswain had timed it all perfectly, and the Waesche dropped back into place just as the SRP penetrated the notch.

Obie widened his stance and crouched lower in the bow. The coxswain glanced around, making eye contact with the SRP retrieval crew on the Waesche. All that was left to do was gun the throttle one last time, so Obie could get the capture line on the horn. But there was no time. The doors were never ordered shut, the Waesche's course was not good, so as the Waesche took an unsuspecting swell from the stern, a wave lifted the SRP and slammed it forward. The capture line and net surged over the bow of the small boat, hitting Obie square in the chest, throwing him aft in the SRP like a rocket. His body slammed against the steering console. As he stood up dazed, he looked around, first towards the fishermen, to make sure they were ok, then towards his coxswain. Slightly shaken and a bit stunned, everywhere he saw foam and spray. He swiped away the moisture from his googles and he could just barely hear his coxswain screaming at him – "Are you OK! Are you OK!" He gave a half assed smile and a thumbs up. Then someone else yelled – "Close those fucking doors! Close the mother fucking doors!" But it was again, too little, too late. A second wave ruptured into the notch, slamming into the SRP harder than before, once again sending it heaving forward. Obie turned to take the full force of the capture net. This time it did not throw him, it followed his body and his head directly into the steering console, shearing it six inches clear of its mount....

Blood began spilling from his googles...

Everything makes me cry. I read the incident reports and witness statements often. They still make me sick. I've included the Coast Guard's *edited* statements in the back of the book and I've included two of Obie's shipmates *unedited* versions in the chapter to come. They are the firsthand accounts. They are the Coast Guard Investigation Reports and the results of FOIA requests. They include the screaming on deck. The blood in Obie's googles. Throwing up. Crying. Traumatized people on deck. Battle Stations. Stunned fishermen. Emergency Flight Ops. IVs. Obie squeezing hands – hanging in there. More blood. They didn't know where the blood was coming from. His eyes? His ears? His stomach? But he was conscious. The entire time, he was conscious. Communicating to the EMT onboard through hand squeezes. Hand squeezes that represented hope and love. "Hang in there buddy."

* * *

THE SRP SMALL-BOAT WOULD BE TOTALED. The operations manual for the National Security Cutters would be re-written. No crew would be allowed to stand in the front of the SRPs anymore. My son would die. Someone would say that *"HE DIED SO OTHERS MAY LIVE."* This phrase would be better heard before the incident as "we fixed the equipment so your son and others may live."

Memorials would be held.
Medals given.
Flowers sent.
Wreaths tossed overboard.
Tears would fall.
Shipmates would speculate.
Commands would frame the story.
Families would fight.
The Deadliest Catch did what it did, you can watch it on Amazon for a nominal fee.

I would never deny. I don't deny. But I would come to get angry. I would search for answers. And I want to hear the stories - the good with the bad. I need to hear it all, I need to know. And I would cry. Oh man would I cry.

* * *

OBIE SURVIVED THAT DAY, though he wasn't expected to live through the night. He was kept alive by one of his close friends, the combat medic aboard that patrol, the medical team and the quick actions of the crew. He made it to Anchorage, and weeks later to Seattle. The men and women of his ship wondered about him, though, as you'll read, were kept at a distance and in the dark. I woke up early on November 12, to a phone call, and to a never-ending day – a day of *Troubled Waters*...

PART 2

Hospitals

VETERANS DAY

November 11, 2013

It was a beautiful day in Idaho where we live. It was so beautiful that I didn't even have a coat on.

—The memories of Laurie Powell

I was outside putting amber-colored (for Thanksgiving) twinkle lights on the Quaking Aspen out in front of our house. All the while I'd been thinking that I wished Obie could be home for Thanksgiving. I missed him so much! Thanksgiving was a very important date for him. You see, he loved Christmas and Thanksgiving marked the day that he could start listening to Christmas music and I would always have the holiday lights up for him as well. We did this from the time that he was little. Give him Christmas lights and Christmas music and he was happy! I knew of course that he couldn't be here for Thanksgiving that year, but I was thinking and hoping that maybe, just maybe, he could come home for Christmas. He was actually going to put in for leave as soon as his command would let him. In all of the years he had been in the Coast Guard, he had not been home once for Christmas. He always held back so that the ones with wives and children could put in for their leave at the holidays. He said they should get the first option because they had families they should be with.

We were emailing back and forth on November 7th and I asked him if he had gotten any word yet as to whether or not he had been approved for leave. He said that he couldn't put in a request until the command figured out the port duty schedule, but that he would let me know as soon as he had word.

Veterans Day brought on a plethora of deep thoughts. I thought of the sacrifices that all of those that serve make, in all branches of the military. I thought of the sacrifices that all who have served have made for their families, and the sacrifices the families have made, too. Being away from home and family for such long periods of time is so stressful on everyone. One must accept not being able to communicate on a regular basis, or even not at all. Sometimes the only way to stay in touch is through email, and that can be frustratingly limited. Loved ones of those in the service always worry and are concerned for their safety.

We all know some suffer and pay the ultimate sacrifice. God Bless them all! As those thoughts ran through my mind, I couldn't imagine how those families must feel, especially on Veterans Day. My heart went out to all of them! I thought of how much I missed Trav and how much I would love to be able to talk to him, I so missed his phone calls. There was no cell service out in the middle of the Bering Sea and he could only call while in port, which didn't happen that often. I wanted to send him an email (I'm regretful I didn't) and tell him "HAPPY VETERANS DAY," but realized how very silly that was. He wasn't a Veteran... I just missed him so much!

I didn't quite get the lights finished before it grew dark, so we went inside for the evening and I thought I would finish them up the following day. I thought about taking a picture of them and sending it to him, but I wasn't sure – it might make him homesick. He would be on liberty by then. I knew they were on their way to Dutch Harbor for a port call, and I could talk to him and find out how his "talk" with the command went.

He had had a huge change of heart throughout this patrol. And in the last email I received from him on the 7th, he said he wanted to talk with his Command once they reached Dutch Harbor. He said in his email "this ship is horrible". I was caught off guard. I realize it's the military, but he had never sounded like that before – it wasn't like him. The morale was really bad on the ship and he had not experienced that type of command before. The crew were made to feel as if they were just expendable resources.

It's not as if he hadn't been on cutters before and experienced life at sea. He was in the Coast Guard for almost 9 years at this point. And no, this isn't "just the way it is on Cutters." In recent conversations and emails, he asked me to check with the Idaho State Police to see if they were hiring and the prices/availability of small homes in Idaho Falls. He said he would work for his dad while he was testing for ISP, until he could get hired, and by doing that, he thought he would be okay financially. He had it all mapped out and hopefully he would be home soon and could start a new life.

But I would shortly find out his ship was diverted that Veterans Day, to assist the Fishing Vessel Alaska Mist. He never made it to Dutch Harbor to have that conversation with his Command. He never made it home!

* * *

AT 4:10 A.M. IN THE EARLY MORNING of November 12th, 2013, my cell phone rang. I knew as soon as I heard it ring that something was terribly wrong - a mom's intuition. My heart sank. The man identified himself as being with the Coast Guard, asked my name and if I was the mother of BM3 Travis R. Obendorf. Once I verified the information, he asked if I had someone there with me, my heart sank even further. He then began to tell me that there had been an accident and that my son had been gravely injured; he was not expected to live. He had been airlifted to Anchorage and the doctors were doing everything possible for him. He was in "severe critical condition." He then said, if the Coast Guard could get us on a flight, we might be able to see him "in time." They couldn't make any promises, but they would do the best they could. I told him that we lived an hour away from the closest airport but that we could be out the door in a matter of minutes, if he could just please get us on the earliest flight! There were a number of phone calls back and forth to get all of the needed information. They were making the necessary arrangements.

One of the phone calls told me that they would only approve flights for three people, and that my husband, Chad, would have to make his own arrangements and fly on his own. They would reimburse him (we didn't really care about that), but he could not travel with me. We weren't in a position to do anything otherwise. I just wanted to get to my son. I know the Coast Guard was trying as hard as they could to get us to Anchorage. Finally, we got verification of my flight and we raced into Idaho Falls.

I called some of my family members to let them know about the situation and asked them to pray, please pray... "Pray like you've never prayed before." Our flight left around 8:00 A.M. Obie's dad, stepmom and myself on board. Chad was able to get a later flight and make arrangements for the care of our animals. Every member of my family pitched in and helped, our friends as well. They were amazing and helped in every way possible.

I never knew that time could go so excruciatingly slow. A layover in Salt Lake City aged me a decade. I had been given a phone number and information for the hospital where they had taken Obie, so I was able to call and get updates. Nothing changed, "just hope and pray that you get here in time." We then flew into Seattle and had another 3½ hour layover, another ten years. We received a phone call asking if some of the Coast Guard Commanders and Chaplain from that area could meet with us while we were waiting for our connecting flight. Of course, we agreed to meet with them. The Coast Guard was really really trying – they were very kind. And besides, what else were we to say? But all the while, I had an overwhelming feeling that something more was going on. They were being very attentive and accommodating and all of them wanted to know what they could do to help us, but we were getting so much attention. Just "make sure my son lives," is all I could say – "that's what you can do for us."

I called the hospital in Anchorage again for updates. No changes. I was hoping for a miracle, praying for a miracle. I asked the nurse to please tell him how very much we love him and to hang on – "hang on baby!"

Finally, we arrive in Anchorage at about 6:30 pm, twelve hours after departing Idaho Falls. Two Coast Guard Officers and a Chaplain met us at our gate. My guard was up once again because something felt very unsettling, despite what was going on with Obie. Call it a mother's instinct. What were his external injuries, I asked the Lieutenant.? I needed to prepare myself for what he might look like. I didn't want to fall apart when I saw him. I needed to stay strong for him. The Lt said: "surprisingly, given his injuries, he looks very good. There are a lot of tubes and wires and he is hooked to a lot of equipment and he's on a ventilator." There was a drain in his brain to help with the build-up of fluid, an abrasion on his head and quite a nasty gash on his hand, "you can actually see the tendons," she said. Otherwise, given his condition and the extent of his injuries, he looked good. We retrieved our bags and were finally in the car. OK! Take us to my boy!

Oh my God. My son! Oh, my beautiful son...those beautiful eyes, that beautiful smile, that infectious laughter, those wonderful hugs. All of these memories came rushing at me and I felt as if I had just hit a brick wall. You are still my beautiful son, but what has happened to you? She was right! He was motionless, tubes, wires and equipment were everywhere. Alarms kept going off. How, could this be happening!!

My Gentle Giant is now fighting for his life. I didn't know what to do! I didn't know how to help him! He couldn't talk, he couldn't open his eyes, he couldn't move and he was not expected to live! How did this happen!

FIGHT FOR YOUR LIFE

A Transition

Quietly optimistic. Obie had some movement in his hands and feet, on command, when off of sedation. "We were really surprised that he made it through that night. There are some good signs", but he was still very much in the "High Danger Zone." That is what the doctors told us when we arrived.

His skull was crushed. He had severe damage to his Brain Stem, severe TBI. Just Hope and Pray - that's all we could do at that point. He was in there. He could hear us, so we were advised to be careful what we said when we were in his room. He was basically trapped within his own body. He couldn't open his eyes, he couldn't move, but he was aware. *"YOU NEED TO PREPARE YOURSELF FOR THE WORST."* We were told that they were doing all they could to help him and make him as comfortable as possible, but there was only so much that could be done. The rest was up to him and his body. "People don't usually recover from an injury like this, just hope and pray." These were the words of the doctors and nurses that were caring for Obie.

At last, Chad finally arrived!

The Coast Guard personnel that met us when we landed stayed with us. They were actually there every day to help us with whatever we needed, and I thank them for everything that they did for us. The Chaplain stayed and they airlifted his Senior Chief off the ship to meet us at the hospital. But I knew in my gut and my heart that something was not right. There was too much attention, too many uniforms.

The Senior Chief's feet no more hit the floor in the ICU unit than I was in his face. I wanted to know "what the hell really happened to my son!" He got emotional trying to tell us, at least as much as he said he knew. He told us that he didn't see it all happen, nor was he really involved in the events. He said that he had watched the footage afterwards and it was "very brutal." He said he heard all of the commotion and came around a corner and saw a guy lying there, covered in blood and thought that it was one of the fishermen that they had rescued, and he said "that poor son of a bitch is in bad shape" and then someone yelled "NO SC, its OBIE!" He said he was shocked. I apologized for my abruptness and gave him a hug. I couldn't imagine what everyone on the ship had gone through.

Still, my inner senses were telling me that something was just not right with all of this. Come to find out, my instincts were correct. The Senior Chief was actually right on the front lines. He was part of the Command that day and sat in on the initial meeting. I think they brought him in for damage control, and I understand why they sent him in particular, he came off as sincere. He was very believable.

The Coast Guard booked us into hotel rooms. Fortunately, the hospital staff allowed Chad and I to stay with Obie in his room. The room right next door was vacant and there were sliding doors that opened between the two rooms, so we opened up the doors. They allowed us to use the room as long as it wasn't needed by someone, which was huge, not something that is normally allowed. The staff found another chair so that we each had one to sleep in and they gathered blankets for us. The staff was amazing. I'm so grateful to them! I could not leave my son!

I was afraid to leave his room, even for a moment, fearing that he might pass away while I was gone.

HOSPITAL JOURNAL

God puts rainbows in the clouds so that each of us – in the dreariest and most dreaded moments – can see the possibility of hope.

—*Maya Angelou*

I STARTED A NOTEBOOK with his progress so that I could read it back to him and he could see what amazing things he had accomplished. "You'll do this!" I said. "You'll make it. I know you will! I know you can do this! I know how strong you are! I know what a strong will you have! You can do this baby......you can do this!"

NOVEMBER 13, 2013

They had told us initially that we all needed to be as quiet as possible while we were in your room. Sounds and noises can make a brain injury patient very agitated because they can hear everything around them but can't see or talk. I told them how much you loved music and asked if I kept it very soft, if I could please play music for you. I thought it would be helpful. I also asked if it would be all right if I applied some essential oils to help keep you calm. I called some friends that verified what oils would be best. One of your RTs (she was awesome) knew of someone that I could get the oils from in Anchorage. I think it helped. I hope it did! I think the staff even enjoyed it. They said it was like entering a spa when walking into your room, with the soft music and the smell of the oils. "Very calming," they said. That's what I was hoping for. I needed to help you in some way, anyway. I just wish I could do more. As a mother, I have never felt so helpless with my child.

It's still a wait, hope and pray situation. You have no pupil eye movement, but "it's encouraging that your eye set is in a forward fixed position, rather than a down fixed position." You have developed pneumonia and you're struggling with blood pressure and temperature fluctuations (this will be ongoing; it is a part of TBI) despite all of the medications they are pumping into you. You are showing more positives as far as hand and feet movement. I was standing next to your bed talking to you and I noticed there was blood coming out of your ear. I grabbed a tissue and asked the nurse about it. She said it was probably just from a sore in your ear, but I knew better; it's because of all of the bleeding in your brain. I knew she had just told me that to try to make me feel a little better. It didn't work, but bless her for trying. Oh, my son....how can I help you!

Summary of what the Brain Stem does: It's one of the most vital regions for the body's survival. The Brain Stem controls the flow of messages between the brain and the rest of the body. It controls functions such as breathing, respiration, reflexes, heart rate, swallowing, blood pressure, vision, hearing, digestion, temperature, consciousness, etc. This just gives you an idea of what you are fighting against.

November 14, 2013

More of the same. Waiting, hoping, praying! SO many people are holding prayer sessions for you. The Coast Guard has been here in full force. I can't keep track of who was who. There is another young man that had arrived to help with the tragedy. He is with Navy Wounded Warrior Safe Harbor. His name is also Chad (and he is wonderful). He brought with him a big binder of information for people with TBI and their caregivers. This would be my homework and I am very grateful for the information. I am grateful to him and his partner (who is in Seattle) because they are offering their help in any way possible and his presence is very calming. He is a very kind man. All of the support is greatly appreciated, but my priority is you.

One of the pilots of the crew that airlifted you off of the ship came to see you today. He is also a wonderful man. I hope I get this right…. He said it was horrible. The weather conditions were insane. When your ship called for the MEDEVAC the weather was so bad that it was looking as if they might not be able to fly. He knew your life depended on it and he was beside himself. He didn't know what to do. He was hoping and praying that something would change because he was afraid they wouldn't make it to you in time. He then thought about his little girl who wanted to be a nun when she grew up and thought if anyone could get through to God, it would be her. So, he told her what he could of the situation and asked her to pray with him. He said within a few minutes the weather improved enough that they were able to take off and get you off the ship. Thank you God and bless this man and his little girl! It was 6.5 hours from the time the MEDEVAC was requested, until the helicopter reached the ship to airlift you. I was also told that the weather was so bad and the swells so high that when the Helo lifted off and raised with you in the basket, the ship was lifted up by a huge wave and slammed the basket into the deck of the ship. What else could have gone wrong!

November 15, 2013

You had to have a transfusion today. The doctors said that due to your injuries and intake of fluids, your body is not responding as it should. What is being reproduced is somewhat diluted because of the high fluid intake they have you on. If I understood that correctly. You can do this baby, keep fighting! I love you my son!

November 16, 2013

The doctor ordered another CT and we got back very positive results compared to the original scan! YES!! The doctors want to wait and do another scan on Tuesday. Depending on the results, they might start backing off on your sedation and use of the drain. If you do well with that then the rest of the tubes can possibly come out. The 4th Ventricle is still blocked, but we are thinking positively! You're fighting SO hard! Tonight, is a rough night for you. They are trying to keep your temperature and blood pressure in check and moving you every hour to prevent bed sores and skin breakdown. You had tears running down your cheeks at one point when they were trying to move you. I had wiped them from your cheek the previous day and it broke my heart. I can't begin to imagine what you're going through. It has to be so painful, frustrating and confusing. You're a prisoner in your own body! One day you're vibrant and alive, helping save lives and making plans for your future. And now THIS! You have done so well, though. No one on the ICU floor can believe what you've accomplished! I wish I could help you! I wish I could trade places with you! You're so young and such an amazing person. You have so much of your life ahead of you. You had all of your plans put into place! Just keep fighting baby! I love my son, so very much!

November 18, 2013

I missed a day, the 17th. I'm not sure why. I'm not sure what took place. I apologize.

You had another scan today and you accomplished some amazing things again! You're still fighting with temperature control and blood pressure. This will be an ongoing battle given your injuries. But you still stunned the ICU floor again today. Nurse J (your admissions nurse) got a strong handshake from you on both sides! He asked if you were in pain and you shook your head no (OMG). He then asked if you could see the light when it was shown in your eyes and you shook your head YES......OH MY GOD, OH MY GOD! Are all of our prayers being answered? Not only did you respond to a direct question, it also meant that you experienced light recognition. HUGE!! Is the miracle that we have been asking for happening? You're so amazing! You're fighting SOOO hard! You have even sat up in your chair. You've crossed your legs in the lotus position (on your own), your favorite way to sit! You even tried to rise up from your bed. That didn't go so well, but it was pretty amazing to see you try. This is all so amazing and wonderful! Thank you, thank you, and thank you!

November 19, 2013

The medical team did another scan today. The 4th Ventricle is starting to open so they are talking about the possibility of levelling off your drain. You've backtracked a little on your nutrition intake, however. You're not absorbing again, so you're on different antibiotics. They have slowed down a bit on your feeding, and that's not good in the respect that they have said nutrition is one of the most important ingredients in healing a brain injury. They are also changing your sedation medication because you're starting to develop some liver issues. You're having a rough night. I wish I could help you! I wish I knew what to do! I love you Trav! Keep fighting!

November 20, 2013

The doctors ordered another scan today. Dr. B, the neurologist, is concerned about blood in an area of the brain that was not noticed before. They want to rule out an aneurysm! An MRI is the only way to accurately determine if there is in fact an aneurysm, but the neurologist refused to do one because of the severity of your injuries. He felt it would be too dangerous. If I am understanding this correctly, it has something to do with how they have to position you in order to do the MRI that would be too dangerous and there is potential to do even more damage to the brain stem. Instead, they performed numerous CT scans and dissected them in a number of ways to try and rule out their suspicions. Once again, time stood still! Results are back! They determined that there is NOT an aneurysm!! Amazing news! And more good news—they removed your respirator. You my son are breathing a 100 percent on your own! But you're not having a very good night however, despite all.

November 21, 2013

You're very agitated today! You did sit up in the chair for a while. But back in bed now and VERY agitated. SHIT! Oh My God... I just discovered the source of your agitation. I thought that you had just relieved yourself (BM), so I lifted up your gown to check and make sure before I called for the nurse. Your lap and bed were covered with blood and blood clots. The source of the blood and blood clots, I found out later, was your day-nurse who had decided on her own to change out your catheter. Well, she couldn't get it to go in right so she just forced it, and in doing so, forced it through your prostate wall. You laid here all day, in pain, bleeding internally, and building up massive blood clots! Massive is not an overstatement. As I said, the way you were bearing down, I thought you were struggling with a bowel movement, but that was not the case. You were trying to pass massive blood clots through your catheter! Nurse T and I worked all night to try and help you. She called the urologist and they instructed her to irrigate and try to get the blood clots to break up and clear out. We worked and worked; it didn't help. FINALLY, they took you to do an Ultrasound. That is when they discovered what the Day nurse had done. They rushed you to surgery and re-routed the catheter. I can't begin to imagine how painful that whole episode must have been! They backed off on your drain at 4:00 A.M. and you have another scan scheduled for 8:00 A.M. They are going to see how you handle the pressure. Depending on the results, they are talking about the possibility of taking the drain out! I spoke too soon. There is too much swelling around the brain stem and too much fluid in the cavity. They will re-scan on Monday. They had to take you back into surgery again for the catheter issue. Nurses are doing continuous bladder flushes to try to break-up and clear out all of the blood clots.

November 22, 2013

You're still having catheter problems. I can't imagine how painful this has all been. Your blood pressure is really high. They have changed your meds again and you're resting a little better now. You got to sit in the chair for a while again today, but you gave yourself a bloody nose through your agitation. This battle is breaking my heart! I wish I could help you baby! You pulled your feeding tube out. You can't keep your feet and legs on the bed. I think you're trying to escape and I can't blame you a bit! I no more put your feet back on the bed than you move them back off to the side. I know you want out of here! Hopefully, you will rest well this weekend. You're resting better right now, but you have developed another fever. We keep switching back and forth with the heating and cooling blankets. Your dad and I have been talking about all of the issues amongst ourselves as well as with the people that are still here with us, CH and the other Coast Guard personnel. Your dad wants you moved to another hospital. He's very angry with the problems that have occurred. I am frustrated and feel helpless, but grateful at the same time. They have taken amazing care of you overall, but it's just really scary for us. There have been issues and problems, yes. They didn't have to accept you here, but they did. The bigger problem is that there is not a hospital in Alaska that has Level 1 Trauma care, not to mention how dangerous it could be to move you. And, sadly, there are always issues with medical care. I hate to say that but it's almost always true. We don't know what it might be like somewhere else. I'm NOT dismissing anything, nor blaming anyone. It is just a fact, a sad fact! Your dad and I have decided to talk to the doctors about all of this.

November 23, 2013

Your dad and I had a meeting of the minds today with both of your doctors. We voiced our concerns regarding your care and they were on it. They changed your blood pressure meds and antibiotics again. They changed your anxiety meds. They took blood from all areas of entry to try to find out where the infection is coming from. You're losing more weight and struggling with nutrition issues. Oh, my son, I wish I knew what to do! You are growing that beard that you always wanted. I just wish you could see it! You can do this, baby! You've got this! You're resting well so far tonight. You had a big day with all of the additional testing that they did. Your dad and I decided that we would follow a set schedule, 12/12's. He's day and I'm night, which is fine because that's really what we've been doing anyway....and I can't leave you! I love you baby!

November 24, 2013

You're experiencing more clotting from the catheter issue. GOD, this has to be so incredibly painful! Your nurse and I tried for some time to irrigate and break up the clots. They finally called the urologist again and he also tried for quite a while to break up the clots. He finally gave up and decided to take you back to surgery AGAIN to remove the clots, cauterize the prostate wall wound and put in a different catheter! Oh my God, you have struggled with this for long enough. Now that the procedure is done, you seem to be resting peacefully. You have to be worn out! I can't imagine all of the pain......and I'm really worried about what it did to your head injuries with bearing down and the pressure from trying to pass all of those clots! I'm worried, really worried. They will do another scan in the morning. It's about 9ish and you're getting a little restless.

November 25, 2013

They shut your drain off at 4:00 A.M. again. They close it off prior to the new scans to see how your brain handles the pressure from all of the fluid. If you do well, you will be able to get it out at some point! Let's hope things are looking better! I'm concerned given what you have already been through with the catheter issues. Nope, spoke too soon.

You still have horns instead of butterflies. That's how they explained it to us. What a visual that creates! They will re-scan on either Wednesday or Thursday to see if there is any progress. Dr. B is optimistic but he said we might be looking at having to put in a VP shunt, which is a permanent, internal drain in the brain. You are having a very restless and agitated day and night. I know there is A LOT of confusion and frustration. I can't IMAGINE! You are aware of everything that is going on around you. You can hear everything that everyone is saying. Sometimes some people forget this. Given everything that has happened to this point, you are still doing amazing things! You mumbled "mom" and "I love you, mom" tonight. It took a lot of encouragement from Nurse T and I (Nurse T is also amazing), but how wonderful it was to hear! You are amazing my son! I love you so much! Your awesome shipmates sent you a get-well card! Pretty cool! You are my hero. You always have been!

November 26, 2013

You slept soundly for the first time, from midnight, it's now 7:00 A.M. and you're beginning to stir. It was so good to see them get you in the chair. I got to see it first-hand! I haven't been able to see you in the chair because they always do that during the day. What a site! AWESOME! I hate having to leave you. Your dad said that you stayed in the chair for 4½ hours. You must have gotten worn out; you slept like a baby all night. You're still fighting a fever. I'm feeling uneasy, concerned and worried. Something doesn't feel right.

November 27, 2013

It sounds like they'll get you in the chair again today. It has to feel so good getting out of that bed! The nurses have talked about the need to get you into a rehabilitation center. They are concerned about skin and muscle issues. We will hope for a good CT scan in the morning. You were in the chair again for about 4½ hours today, but your dad said that you were pretty restless. You're still pretty restless tonight, but you're sleeping like a baby now. This is good. They will clamp your drain at 4:00 A.M. and take you for your CT scan at 8:00 A.M. Keeping our hopes up for a good one! Hope and Pray ~ Hope and Pray! I love you, baby!

November 28, 2013 ~ Thanksgiving Day

The scan results are back. Dr. B thought he saw some improvement but still doesn't want to pull the drain. They will do another scan on Sunday. You sat in the chair for about four hours today and now you're sleeping really well. Healing, I hope. Preparing your body for the next phase. The next chapter in the Journey of Your Life. You've got this, baby! Keep going, keep fighting! SC will be leaving tomorrow. I'm not sure what your Dad is going to do. He and SC have quite a bond. They have become good buddies. He has been very helpful, driving us wherever and whenever, doing our laundry a couple of times. He even bought a speaker for my phone, for your music. Am I grateful for his assistance! We developed somewhat of a friendship, as well, but not like your dad. I have to admit, I thought it strange that the Coast Guard kept him here this long. I don't think this is routine by any means. Your dad and I have had several invitations for Thanksgiving dinner from some of the nurses, even the Coast Guard and again, I am very grateful for the kindness and generosity. We are surrounded by a lot of very kind people. There is no way I can leave you, though. If you have to spend Thanksgiving in the hospital, that is exactly where I am going to be, right here with you! Hey...and we get to start listening to Christmas music! Happy Thanksgiving baby ~ I love you with all of my heart!

November 29, 2013

SC left this morning. He has been here for about two-and-a half-weeks. I checked into the Springhill Inn Suites last night. It's only four minutes away from the hospital, walking distance! That's huge. I hated being as far away as I was. This way I can just run right next door if need be, or of course just walk, HA HA. Your dad decided to stay at the

Hilton for now—spoke too soon. He just called to say that he is moving into Springhill tomorrow. This will be much better, much closer. You sat in the chair again today for about four, almost five hours, your dad said. AWESOME! You're resting peacefully now. We need to get your arms and legs moving! I asked them what they were going to do about your jaw. Oh yes, your jaw was broken as well, not surprising given what happened, but they haven't done anything with it yet. I'm not sure but I'm wondering if they forgot about it. Does that happen? Everything else was of much more importance, obviously. They were going to check into it. Of course, you're still on a feeding tube, but I'm thinking that pretty soon you'll be wanting some of your favorite Shrimp Teriyaki and Flank Steak, so we need to get your jaw fixed! How's that for positive thinking? You slept through the night; you were a little restless but better than most nights. In the wee hours you had a coughing spell and the RT came in to clean out what you had coughed up with a suction device. You have a Respiratory Therapist helping you (she's great). Actually, you have two (they are both great). They have allowed me to help with suctioning because you're having trouble with swallowing, so the mucus and phlegm gets built up. If it's not suctioned, you choke, and it builds up frequently.

I am concerned about your drain. It looks to me like it might be clogged. There are two little granules (brain matter) in the tube that haven't moved for a while. I mentioned it to the nurse and she was going to show it to the doctor. I also mentioned it to your dad so that he could keep an eye on it. He also talked with them about it. They think that it's okay, that the granules probably moved and we didn't notice and these are just new ones that have collected. We asked about the fluid output of the drain and they admitted that it had diminished somewhat, but that it had before and it's nothing to be concerned about. I'm not convinced, but they are the medical professionals. What can we do? How do we know? Nurse J (female), the day nurse, is also amazing. She is here for the morning shift. They change out at 6:30. She started doing some exercise movements with you and you just took off from there! It was pretty amazing! It had to feel SOOO good to be able to move! I can't imagine how much you have missed that. It had to be driving you crazy! You lived in the gym. Well, your dad is here now, so I have to leave. I love you, my son. I'll see you tonight.

November 30, 2013

You're still sleeping like a baby. Almost too quiet. I'm a little concerned, a lot concerned actually, or maybe I'm just being a mom. I know you have to be exhausted and the best thing for healing is rest. Sleep is good! But I'm concerned. You're really struggling with swallowing. Okay, you're starting to roust. You're doing more on command; they are working with you on resistance exercises! You sat in the chair again for a good while and you're resting well tonight. They are turning off your drain again at 4:00 A.M. to get ready for your next scan at 8:00 A.M. This one will determine if you get a clean break from the drain or if you have to get a permanent VP Shunt put in. We'll keep our fingers crossed! Hope & Pray ~ Hope & Pray! I love you my son.

December 1, 2013

A new day, a new month, hopefully some really good news! When I was using the suction to help you, I discovered what looked like a great big piece of hamburger on the roof of your mouth. Well, we all know that you haven't been eating hamburger, so of course I'm alarmed, knowing that it's something that shouldn't be there. I brought it to the attention of the nurse. She said, "OOooo, that doesn't look good" and said she would ask the doctor. I also mentioned how dry your mouth was because of the open mouth breathing. Nurse J (your male nurse) happened to come by to check on you. He was your nurse at admission, the first one to take care of you and I really, really like him. He's amazing! So, I thought it was the perfect opportunity...I'll ask him. I showed him the roof of your mouth. "Oh, my yes," were his words. It's from poor oral care. They weren't cleaning out your mouth properly so all the plaque grows, builds up, and it has adhered to the roof of your mouth. I was stunned, of course. I had never heard of such a thing, or seen anything like it! So, he reached in and tried to pry out what he could. He told the other nurses that you needed liquid saliva and humid air, not to mention better oral care! So, they got you hooked up with a humidifier and finished cleaning out the yuck. SHIT Man, what's next? The scan results are back. No go. Dr. B say's that you need an internal, permanent, VP Shunt and it's up to us as to whether they do it here or in Palo Alto.

I need to catch up on details, I've been slacking.

They told us that they have done all that they can for you here in Alaska. We have had several discussions as to where the best place might be for your long-term rehabilitation. You will probably have to re-learn how to walk and talk among many other challenges. Chad H and the Coast Guard have been helping us with considerations for different facilities. We have a few options but some are so far away from Idaho. So.... Palo Alto Polytrauma Rehabilitation Center was an option and we have reached out to them with the help of LT. O, CH, CWO and many others that are helping to coordinate all of this. It is in California. You could be close to your friends from the ship. They could come and visit, and help give you encouragement. It would be the closest to Idaho so it would be easier for family and friends to come and visit, too. I would go with you and stay, learning what I need to know in order to take care of you once you graduated from there and we'd get to take you back home. I am still studying the binder that Chad H. gave me, but this would be hands-on training. It just all makes the most sense. They still have to accept you, of course, but it sounds very promising.

Since there has been talk of transferring you, I started taking pictures of your nurses/doctors with you. I've also begun collecting their contact information so that we can keep them up to date with your progress. You have stolen the hearts of the ICU staff. They have never seen anyone overcome what you have, or encountered anyone with such a strong will who fights so hard against the odds. They want to stay in touch with you. You haven't been able to see any of these wonderful people that have been caring for you, so by having a picture to identify with, once you open those beautiful blue eyes, you will be able to relate to who we will be talking about.

I also forgot to mention, quite some time ago, that both Chad and your stepmom had to return to Idaho Falls and get back to work. I lost track of when they had to leave. I apologize for that. We've been keeping them updated and they have been passing the information along to family and friends. I've tried to keep up with this, but my focus has just been on you and your progress! You are amazing, my Rockstar! I love you, my son!

Okay, I think I have everything caught up, so back to the decision of whether or not to have the shunt put in here, in Alaska, or in California. Your dad had a good thought. He said that it might be a good idea to wait and have the VP Shunt surgery done in Palo Alto and we could possibly get a second opinion. We've all talked about it and think that this would be the best direction for you, if it's an acceptable option. So, we will wait and see what Palo Alto has to say. After having this discussion, your dad and I walked back into your room and the doctor was taking apart your drain (that's in the brain). We asked him what was going on, what was happening? He said he was taking it apart to unclog it! So, it has been clogged for the last two days! OMG! We had tried to tell them and they wouldn't listen. I wonder what that has done to your condition. Why is all of this happening? You are fighting so hard to live.

Nurse G. (very nice lady) called and met with us this evening. She is a nurse at The TBI Clinic. She brought us some wonderful food items that she had made and a beautiful Christmas tree that she made just for you. She talked with your nurses and one of your doctors, took some notes and is going to help get you to Palo Alto as well. She offered her help and support in any way that she could. The weird part is that it really pissed everyone off, including the CG, and they are the ones that asked her to come. What I understood from all of it, the commotion and the hubbub, was that she asked TOO many questions, so they told her not to come back again. I was confused. I thought she was very knowledgeable and helpful. HHMMMM. This I found very unsettling. In fact, she had had a severe brain injury herself and had recovered. But, again, what do I know? You got up in the chair again today and now resting really well. I hope that's what is going on, that you're just getting rest! We hope that you will be in Palo Alto by the end of next week.

December 2, 2013

It was a very quiet day for you other than getting in the chair. You slept well all night. You were very quiet and I have a very uneasy feeling. You got a nice bath at about 4 A.M. that had to feel good and probably helped you to sleep a little better, maybe. They are still working on arrangements for Palo Alto but there is still lots of planning that needs to take place. Sleep well baby ~I love you, my son!

December 3, 2013

Everyone is still working on the planning and coordinating for Palo Alto. All of the doctors need to talk to one another. Otherwise, you're still very quiet. I'm concerned, I'm very concerned. I'm hoping that your body is just healing. Twenty-three days today have passed since this tragedy. For twenty-three days, you have been fighting to live against the odds, against all odds. I can't wait for you to open those beautiful eyes and call me "Shithead" again. I can't wait to hear that laugh and get one of those great big bear hugs. I love you so much, Trav. I can't believe all of this has happened. I wish I knew what to do. I just wish I could take all of this away. I wish I could trade places with you! This is not right. NONE of this is right!

You yawned tonight, or was it a moan? I have not seen you do that since we have been here. I will try to think of it as a good sign. Dr. C stopped by at about midnight. I really like him. He's a very kind man. His son was severely injured in the service as well, God Bless Him! He asked if Dr. B had stopped by and I told him that I had not seen him. He said that there was a problem with Palo Alto. The doctors are fighting over the VP shunt procedure. They don't want to accept you without the shunt in place and Dr. B won't put in the shunt and then ship you out, which is greatly appreciated, but it also means that it would delay you getting started with your rehab, which is becoming a concern with everyone. Dr. B would want to see you through the recovery from the shunt procedure, he said he would want to keep you for another couple of weeks. We have been told that the hospital part of the facility in Palo Alto is civilian and the rehab part is VA. WOW!! Oh my God, how do you know what to do? How do you know if you are making the right decisions? MJ (one of the nurses) came in and gave you a back rub. That was just the ticket. You moved your forehead and your eyebrows. If I didn't know better, I might have thought that you were flirting with her. HA, well knowing you, you probably were in the best way that you could. Nurse D helped you with sign language tonight and you signed "I love you," with his help of course. "I LOVE YOU, BABY, more than you will ever know!" I've been thinking about needing to learn sign language in case you're not able to speak. We can learn together (in fact I have a book at home). But you'll need to be able to open your eyes so you can see sign language. One step at a time. Palo Alto…It will all fall into place once we get you there and they start working with you. OMG! This is wonderful. You are sitting cross-legged again!

December 4, 2013

Well, we finally got word about Palo Alto. They will not accept you without a VP Shunt in place. So, they will do another scan in the morning and either there will be some improvement, which is what we are praying for, and the drain will come out, or you will need a shunt. Either way, you cannot be transported for two days after the drain is removed, or for two weeks after the shunt placement. You sat in the chair again today. You seem pretty tuckered out tonight. We will see what answers morning will bring. Hope and Pray. Hope and Pray. I love you, baby.

December 5, 2013

You have been down for your scan. Now we will wait and see what the doctors say. To shunt or not to shunt. Well, word is back. Definitely shunt. This scan was much worse than the last one. They actually consulted and got three opinions; all had the same conclusion. VP Shunt surgery will be at 7:40 in the morning. Chaplain L will be here at 7:00 A.M. to have a prayer with us prior to surgery and this will be the beginning of a new leg of your journey. Nurse K (amazing nurse) scrubbed out your mouth really well and you are hooked up and ready to go! Rest well, baby, tomorrow will be a big day. You drained 10 every hour and then they zeroed the drain in prep for the shunt surgery in the morning. I love you my son, with all of my being!

December 6, 2013

This is the day baby! You will have a permanent drain in your brain and hopefully within a couple of weeks we will be on our way to Palo Alto for your long-term rehab. And then HOME! We just need to get you well enough to get you home! You have been through so much! Dr. B will be in first thing and flush you with antibiotics again before surgery.

WHOA, back-up! Dr. B just came in, dressed in scrubs and ready to go, it appeared. He said that he had just spoken with a friend of his who is a "world renowned doctor" practicing in Seattle. His name is Dr. D. He has a procedure called a Third Ventriculostomy, and that you are a candidate for it. Dr. D said that he would accept you if we wanted to try that route. Otherwise, it would be the VP Shunt here in Alaska and two weeks of recovery. After much deliberation, we all decided to try the world-renowned doctor in Seattle. Chad H is in Seattle. JJ is in Seattle, and it's closer to Idaho. It just seemed like the right direction to go. Again, how do you know for sure?

So, now we are back to a lot of rushed planning. Everyone was amazing and jumped in. The hospital is calling Guardian Life Flight to arrange for pilots and nurses to transport you. The Coast Guard are doing what they do for arrangements and clearances. Chad H and FE are working their magic. It all took a while but they got it done. Now we just have to wait for Life Flight to get here to pick us up. Your dad told me that I could fly with you. Only one of us could go on the plane because it's so small. The Coast Guard would get a flight for him to follow.

It seemed like hours (it was quite a few, actually), but they finally arrived to get us. They told me to take something very warm because it would probably be pretty cold on the flight. They would need to keep it colder to begin with, given your condition, because heat is one of the worst things for a brain injury. I asked if I could borrow a blanket from the hospital. They all laughed and said that I could keep it. I did keep it; I still have it. I'm not sure why it was something that I have held onto, other than it represented a glimmer of hope on that day. Hope, that this move would be the answer to our prayers. Our son might make it, he might get better and we might be able to take him home. Everyone said their good-bye's, wished us all the best and asked us to stay in touch. We told them all how grateful we were for everything that they had done for us. I had all of their contact information so we could keep them updated. We had to leave the Christmas tree that Nurse G had made for you, but I took some of the decorations off so that you would have them for remembrance. I still have those as well.

Man, they weren't kidding. It was cold! The windows frosted over. I had my coat on and the blanket that they gave me and it was still freezing, but that's okay. If that's how it needed to be for you, it's all good! I kept turning around to see how you were doing. It was a very small plane and noisy, so I couldn't talk to the nurses. I just kept turning around and they would give me a thumbs up. After a while it started to warm up. I even took my coat off at one point, and then it got really hot. I wasn't sure what was happening. I was concerned but no one said anything. Then I heard the machine go off. The machine that they had you hooked up to made the Flat Line noise and my heart sank! I turned around and they were working on you. They didn't even see me. They didn't say anything. They just kept working on you. I prayed. I still don't know what happened. One of the flight nurses wanted to talk to me when we landed in Seattle and I told her I would come to the waiting room as soon as I could. Everything was so chaotic at first, I couldn't talk to her right then, once I had the opportunity, and went to the waiting room, they had already left. I understand. They were in demand. It haunts me to this day what she needed to tell me, what had happened. I tried to track her down after I had some of my senses back, but was unsuccessful. Maybe it was best that I didn't know.

But here we are. Chad H was here waiting for us to arrive. He had some food waiting for me. He is so amazing! They brought us up to the ICU floor with you on the gurney ahead of us. We came around the corner in the direction of your room and I saw that the room number was exactly the same as the room number in Alaska. I stopped dead in my tracks and said to Chad H, "Oh, my God, his room number is the same. This can't be good." It made me sick to my stomach. Don't ask me why. I just had a really, really bad feeling!

Then they wheeled you off for x-rays and scans and started asking me questions, so many questions. My head was spinning! They brought you back to your room and started poking and pinching saying "unresponsive" again, "unresponsive". I tried to tell them that all they had to do was to talk to you, just ask you to do whatever they wanted. I explained that you could respond to all communication/commands. I tried to talk to them and tell them all of the amazing things that you had accomplished in Alaska, how well you had done, but they just brushed me off and said it had no bearing, that they were doing their own assessment at this point. I was sick. I could see what was happening, I could see what they were doing! It felt as if they were just writing you off! It seemed as if they didn't want to waste their time on you. That's what it felt like. I was helpless and it was hopeless. I didn't know what to do. They wouldn't listen to me! If anything, knowing you as I do, I think you were pissed at them! I could feel you saying, "hey asshole, trade places with me and let me see if you can feel this! Let me twist and pinch your skin until it bruises. Let me stick needles in your feet and see how it feels. No, I'm not going to let these assholes know that it hurts. Let them look at what I've already been through. I can take this! Why don't they read my fucking charts? I've been through Hell and Back and they want me to flinch when they pinch me, NOT happening! And my mom is over there trying to tell them everything and they won't even listen to her! Assholes, Fuck Em!" I was sick. I could not get them to listen. I realize that some of this was necessary and this is the way they test, but it just seemed as if they would have listened to some of what I had to tell them, that it could have spared you some grief. OH, MY God I hope we made the right decision! CH was there in the room with me. I looked at him and said "they won't listen. What do I do? We couldn't do anything; they are the doctors!

Chad H had arranged for rooms on the 5th floor of the hospital for your dad and me, which was wonderful because we could be right there with you. They have rooms there for people that are having treatments, can't travel and have nowhere else to stay. It's a wonderful thing that they offer. They are very inexpensive so people on limited funds can afford them. It's awesome that they have them there for people. I didn't stay in mine. I used the shower and my bags stayed on my bed. I stayed with you; I couldn't leave you. You are hooked up for the night. Nurse H is taking care of you tonight and she is doing a great job!

We thought we were doing the absolute best possible thing for you, yet what we actually did, unknowingly, was deliver you right to death's door!

December 7, 2013

It's Saturday and the weekend doctor came in to see you. He said they would monitor your drain output throughout the day and go from there. Then Dr. D came in to see you. The "world renowned doctor!" What an Asshole! He looked at you and ordered an MRI. If I remember correctly, your dad had to ask him who he was. He just walked in and started talking. He didn't even introduce himself. It was as if we were supposed to know who he was. He said that you were not a candidate for his procedure, and that there is something else going on and he needed to find out what it was. I told him that the doctor in Alaska (his friend) would not do an MRI because it was too dangerous. He said he didn't care; it was the only way to find out[6]. I get it, but it made me sick to my stomach as to what it might mean for you.

The MRI is back. Dr. D said that he needs to look at the brain stem further and something is wrong with the carotid artery. There is too much pressure on the brain, which is from too much fluid. They will do another MRI on Monday and put the VP Shunt in. Then he left. That was it. He was not a pleasant person by any means. Not only was the experience with Dr. D not very pleasant, but you have a new nurse tonight, Nurse V. He took very good care of you medically, but when he had some down time, he decided to have a discussion with me. He sat down in one of the chairs in your room and proceeded to tell me that we needed to start thinking about what was best for you in the long run. He told me we had to think about making some very hard decisions. "The Decision." He proceeded to tell me that this is not the way you would want to live (he doesn't even know you) and that it was not fair to you to continue to suffer. He said that he himself had to make "the decision" twice to let family members go, but that he knew it was the best thing for them. WHAT THE FUCK! Is this really happening! We have only been here for two days. We don't even know for sure what is going on! I don't even know this person. How can he be saying these

---

[6] It was noted in Obie's medical chart that I read after his death that there was additional damage done that might have been due to the MRI.

things to me, and in front of you? Is this even allowed? Do nurses have the authority and the right to have these types of conversations with family members? STOP! STOP, NOW! I'm sick. This is all a Fucking Nightmare! I'm so shocked and stunned and sick I can't even tell anyone. No one would believe me. This is all a NIGHTMARE!

JJ and one of your cousins who lives in Seattle came up to see you and spent the afternoon. It was really nice to see them; I just wish the circumstances were different. Tomorrow will be a coast day for you, which is good. You need one. You've been through so much. Pinching, poking, and talking about you and your condition and you could hear it all. I hated this day. I hate all of this! I can't imagine what you're feeling or thinking. You must be terrified. I love you, baby. I wish I could erase all of this or trade places with you. This is all so VERY wrong!

December 8, 2013

Your dad and I moved over to a different hotel today. There is a shuttle that will take us back and forth from the hospital to the hotel. Chaplain L came to see you. He was the Chaplain that was in Alaska when we first got there. Chad H and FE also came to see you today. They all helped us move our things to the new hotel. Everyone in this network of people has been so amazing! I really don't know what we would have done without all of their knowledge and support. They will start getting you ready for the shunt procedure in the morning. Rest easy baby, tomorrow will be a big day.

December 9, 2013

Your VP Shunt is in. Your external drain is gone and you are resting peacefully right now. They want to do an Angiogram at 3:00 this afternoon to see if they can find out what's wrong with the carotid artery. They also want to put a permanent feeding tube in as soon as possible. I know this all needs to be done in order for Palo Alto to accept you, but it just seems as if they are rushing everything. You don't have time to recover from one thing and they cut your feeding off again to get you ready for another.

JJ came up and spent the day as well as Chad H and Chaplain L. She brought TWO Christmas trees.....not just one, but TWO. My Little Drummer Boy (your favorite Christmas song) that loves Christmas! It was awesome! One of the trees shoots little snowflakes. It's like a perpetual snow globe. You always loved snow globes. All of the nurses want it. I keep that one on at night. It's very peaceful to watch. I wish you could see it as well. The other tree is only on loan. We can't have it, so don't even think about it, Mr. Christmas! Just kidding. This is awesome! She also brought with her a Santa music box that you used to play with when you were little. You always loved music boxes. It's starting to look pretty festive in here! I brought your Rudy Reindeer (you always liked Rudy) that I bought for you in Alaska and now he has company and YOU have Christmas Deco's!

December 10, 2013

Chaplain G came to see you today. He is one of the people that met us at the Seattle airport on our way to Alaska. He hung with your dad for a while and they connected over lots of fishing talk. In fact, as a result, he brought your dad some smoked salmon one day when he came to visit. They did the Angiogram today and found what they called a "very large diffuse aneurysm" at the base of the skull in the carotid artery. They think that the force of the hit, from when the injury occurred, sheared off the carotid artery and it has resulted in a very large aneurysm. It is now 22mm. So, there was one there after all, this whole time! Oh my God! I think I'm sick! They want to do surgery tomorrow and put in a stent. They are puzzled as far as everything else that is going on with your condition. One step at a time. I feel fortunate (I think), or at least we've been told that we should feel fortunate, to have the team of doctors that we do. They are supposed to be the best, right? "World-renowned." Don't get me wrong. Some of them are wonderful, but some, not so much! We just got word that the feeding tube will be on hold for now. The stent is the top priority. Rest well sweetheart. Tomorrow is another big day! I love you with all of my heart!

December 11, 2013

WOW…. OKAY! Crazy day! They wanted to do the stent surgery and put in the feeding tube today. They ended up not being able to do either. In order to do the stent surgery, they have to pump your system with massive amounts of aspirin and Plavix to thin the blood. They call it "loading," which is pretty scary because this also means that it greatly increases bleeding potential. The problem is that you are too responsive to the Plavix, so they have to re-group and get the feeding tube inserted possibly on Friday. The stent surgery is now scheduled for Monday.

Dr. D walked into your room and told us that you would need to go to a nursing home before you could go to rehab. That was it, nothing else. He just walked in, looked at you and said that, then walked out. I feel as if he just wants you out of here. I felt as if he didn't want you here when we first arrived. Anyway, we have stepped things up, re-grouped and Palo Alto has accepted you for both the hospitalization side as well as rehab! No nursing home. Not happening on our watch! So, hopefully, if all goes well, we will be headed to Palo Alto possibly next week. It has been one month to the day since this all began. Rest well, baby. We'll get this figured out!

December 12, 2013

Coast day for you. We thought you would get your stomach tube today but your platelets are still too high, so maybe tomorrow. The problem is you still get no nutrition. They keep cutting off your feeding with the expectation that they will take you into surgery, then it doesn't happen. So, they say, maybe tomorrow. And they still don't give you any nutrition! You have lost almost a pound a day since you've been here. This is on top of what you had already lost. My Gentle Giant is shrinking. We had some discussions with nurses about the doctors. We were getting pretty frustrated. It felt as if Dr. D just wanted us gone, that he had already given up on you. Sadly, the nurses don't have anything good to say about Dr. D either. God, I hope we have made the right decision. This is all so VERY hard!

We found out more information regarding Palo Alto and we are at least feeling better about that. Tensions are high. Things are starting to fall into place, though. We just have to be patient. The brain takes time and the injury was so severe. You're getting closer, baby. Hope and Pray. Hope and Pray. I love you, my son!

December 13, 2013

The doctors took blood at 4:00 A.M. Another MRI was taken this morning at 5:00 A.M. The blood draw is to test to see if your platelet levels have stabilized in order to perhaps place your stomach tube and the MRI is to see if they need to adjust your shunt. Well, the blood results came back and they still can't do the tube. You're still too reactive and you still can't get any nutrition! I don't understand this. The doctors in Alaska said that nutrition is critical for TBI patients and that the lack of it would make things even more dangerous and serious! I even know this. This is all so scary! I feel so helpless! I wish I could do something to help you!

Dr. G (she was amazing) came in to check on you and held your eyelids open, asking if you could see her. You gave her a thumbs up! See, they just need to give you a chance. Just talk to you! I know you can do this. I know you can! Look at the odds you have already beaten. Dr. G then asked me if physical therapy had been in to see you yet. This is the first time anyone has even asked. You have been here for 7 days. What's wrong with these people? I told her no, but that it would be wonderful if someone would come and work with you. You always worked so hard at staying fit, it had to be driving you crazy. So, she asked if you would like that and your foot started moving, wiggling! We both laughed. I couldn't be happier! God Bless this woman! They came in to start working with you right before I left. Awesome! Your room had started to fill up with visitors. Your stepmom has arrived and I thought I had better share.

Okay, gone long enough. I'M BACK! Your dad said that PT/OT did some more testing with your vision and asked if you could see their finger when it started coming from around the side of your head. You could, with both eyes! Just AWESOME! He said that they worked you hard and they were really surprised at your strength and endurance, given what the charts/reports said, which they had read from the doctors' assessments from when you first arrived. They were VERY impressed at what you could do. The doctors hadn't even given you a chance. They didn't even order PT/OT to work with you. Thank God Dr. G asked about it or you still wouldn't be getting it. I can't even begin to explain how I feel right now about some of these doctors. I'm sick and I'm scared at the same time, and I wish I knew more about all of this! I wish I'd asked about PT; I didn't know! You just needed a chance to prove to them what you could do, but they didn't even take the time, nor would they listen. But you did it!! Way to go, Trav! You're so amazing! You're worn out now. Sleep well my son. I love you with all of my heart!

December 14, 2013

Your dad and stepmom arrived with coffee in hand! Yum! Wonderful and Thank you! Rounds with doctors indicated that they would place your stomach tube today, probably in the afternoon. PT and OT therapy came up again today and you rocked the house! You kicked both feet on command, lifted both legs. They are working on getting you to be able to hold your head up and strengthen your core so that they can try to stand you upright. You sat on the side of the bed with assistance, which was SO AWESOME! ROCK STAR!

They came for you at about 2:45 for the stomach tube surgery. We asked them to please try and place it so that it didn't ruin your ship's wheel tattoo. They thought we were kind of silly, but they don't know how important your tatts are to you! You're back now and all went well. It's just on the edge of your tattoo. They did the best they could with placement. Sorry baby, we tried. They gave you some morphine and you're resting well now. You look so much better without the feeding tube in your nose. That looked so uncomfortable and it's been in there for so long, 34 days in fact. Hopefully now they can start getting some nutrition into you. Sounds like we're still on track for Monday for the stent. Maybe Wednesday or Thursday we will be headed for Palo Alto and get you on the road to recovery!

Oh, MY GOD. They just told us that Dr. D cancelled your sessions with PT and OT. He said that they weren't worthwhile. You've got to be fucking kidding me! The therapists were amazed at how well you had done. I don't understand any of this. We have been told that Dr. M is the one that is going to do your stent surgery. I guess Dr. D doesn't have the time to be bothered with it or with you.

December 15, 2013

Oh, my son. You are so amazing! What a fighter! I don't know if it's possible for parents to be prouder of their child. With everything that you've been through, you have fought so hard! You always wanted to be a Hero; well, you are. But, then again, you always have been.

It's a quiet day for you today, which is good. You needed one. They have given you another Plavix and aspirin load. Your dad and stepmom spent the day with you, I did my laundry and tried to take a nap, HA! That didn't happen. They will give you more Plavix and aspirin in a while and test again to see if you get the stent tomorrow. I don't understand this loading process and I have to say that it really, really scares me!

Dr. D has also taken you off of the ICU watch list. It will be every two hours that they rotate you and check everything instead of every hour. Sleep well, baby! The angels are here with you. I was lying with my back to the door of your room and was trying to sleep. I could feel something, so I opened my eyes. When I opened my eyes there was a very soft illuminating light coming from behind me. I was startled at first, I think because I could feel it was something that I couldn't explain. When I got the courage to turn around the sight was unbelievable. There were Angels, too many to count. Small, large, all sizes, all shapes. Very soft illuminating silhouettes all lined up from the head of your bed, out into the hallway. I couldn't believe that the watch nurses weren't seeing them also. How far out of the room they went, I don't know. There were so many, just standing there so patiently, as if standing guard over you, preparing you for what was about to take place. At first, I couldn't believe my eyes. It was such a calm and beautiful sight, and then a part of me realized why they were all there and my heart sank. I was grateful because I could see and feel how well you would be cared for. My heart broke because I knew at that moment that I was going to lose you. You were my gift from heaven and they were there to help you with your journey home. I couldn't sleep the rest of the night. Or did I? Was it just a dream? I told myself, NO, calm down. They were just there to help you through this last surgery. They were there to give you the strength that you needed to make it through this. That's it! That's got to be it! If anyone deserved to have the help of so many beautiful angels it was you! One by one they would stop where your head was resting on your pillow. It was as if they were speaking to you, but only you could hear. I watched them with you for a little bit longer, then I lay my head back down, closed my eyes and prayed even harder than I already had been, and sobbed. When I opened my eyes again, they were gone.

December 16, 2013 – *The Defect, The Deadly Surgery*

They were coming for you first thing in the morning for surgery. Chaplain G and your dad were going to be here early so that we could have a prayer together before they took you to surgery. They were both late. I asked if we could have just a few more minutes, that they both were expected soon. I didn't know what to do. I didn't want them to take you without your dad seeing you first. I wanted a prayer to be said for you by all of us. I scrambled and came up with a prayer that I thought you might like and just as I started to read it beside your bed the doctor came back in. He said it was time, we can't wait any longer. He showed me the authorization form and asked me to sign it. Just as I was ready to sign, your dad and the Chaplain arrived. Your dad said, "Oh no, no, that's for me to sign." So, the doctor handed it to him and told him what he was signing. That's when your dad asked "well, what if something goes wrong?"

The doctor was very matter of fact. "Well," he said, "of course it will mean imminent death." The room went silent. It was deafening and sickening at the same time. They allowed us to have a brief prayer and they took you away. They took my boy away. How can I begin to describe how they brought you back?

It seemed as if time stood still. It did, actually. We were all waiting in your room for them to bring you back from surgery; your dad was there, your stepmom, Chad H and I. It felt like forever until anyone came back into the room to update us. When someone finally came into your room, they didn't have you with them. It wasn't someone bringing you back to your room. It was someone coming for us, retrieving us, gathering us. They told us that Dr. M wanted to meet with all of us in the Family Conference Room. WHAT IS WRONG! WHERE IS MY SON! They wouldn't tell us anything, only that the doctor wanted to meet with us. We all walked very quietly to the conference room and waited for Dr. M to come in. This can't be happening....what is wrong! I was sick and my heart was beating out of my chest!

I remember Dr. M saying, "Something went terribly wrong. There was a "defect on the device." There was a "burr" on it. It burst his aneurysm and he is bleeding out. He is basically brain dead at this point and it will only continue to worsen."

"You are all going to have to make a decision, "THE DECISION" at some point. We will make him as comfortable as possible for now." I don't remember much else, other than UTTER, TOTAL and COMPLETE DESPAIR.

I don't remember walking back to your room after that, but I do remember walking into it and seeing him, my beautiful, amazing son. But it was different this time, it is different. You lay there so very still.

They brought my son back on life support. He could no longer fight for his life as he had been fighting so hard, for so long. Death was consuming him and there was nothing that we could do, nothing that anyone could do to help you.

Most of the equipment and all of the alarms had been turned off, as they were no longer necessary. You are on the ventilator again. So many tubes and wires! You have begun to bleed from your incision from the shunt because of all of the pressure and bleeding in the brain. I kept trying to wipe the blood away but I couldn't keep up with it. I asked them to please try to stop the bleeding. Dr. G (she was wonderful) came in to help. She stitched the incision tighter, the best she could, and put a dressing on it. It helped some. We never saw or heard from either Dr. D or Dr. M again. It was The Nightmare! This was IT!

Then the rest of the Nightmare began. Everyone began to ask questions. Your son had Organ Donor on his records. What do you want to do? How long will you want to keep him on life support? Organ donation will factor into this. Family, you need to contact family. I don't even remember how I did that. I'm not sure that I did. I know I called Chad, I don't remember when or how. I think he made the other necessary calls for me. I really don't remember. He arranged to get on a flight as soon as possible so that he could see you before we had to let you go. THE NIGHTMARE! Commotion, commotion, commotion.....Decisions, decisions, decisions .... Spinning, swirling.... this can't be happening! Now time is going too quickly; much too quickly!!

Why can't you stay with us? Why can't this all be a great big misunderstanding? The nightmare. Just let it be a nightmare and wake me up! You have fought so hard to live...now THIS!! Why was it happening? How could this have happened! You were three days away from Palo Alto, three days away from the road to recovery, the next leg of your Journey. And now you are dying, or in their terms, you are already dead. Your brain is dead, which means you are dead. The machines will keep you breathing and your heart pumping until we can make the "decisions" necessary. How does one do that? How do people do that?

The Organ Harvesting people arrived, it seemed almost immediately. I understood. Time is of the essence. They told us everything that we needed to know regarding the process and what takes place. It was overwhelming. It was all happening too fast. There were too many things to think of, too many things to decide and it was all WRONG! Obie had gone through so much already; gone through so much! He fought so hard to live. Now we are having to decide when we are going to end his life after trying so hard to save it. OH MY GOD!

We still had to make the decision about Organ Donation. It was one of the most difficult decisions, other than ending Obie's life. Those were his wishes and I wanted to honor that. I know that by giving/donating, it could mean saving and enhancing the lives of possibly numerous other people. However, there were also a number of factors involved. In order to donate organs, we would have to keep him on life support for an added amount of time, a fairly substantial amount of time, because of OR availability, according to the doctors. All of that aside, it still had to be our decision. I talked with the Harvesters. I talked with his nurse, Nurse K, and she was wonderful. It all still seemed so unreal, so I went out to the doctor's station where one of the doctors was charting notes. I asked him, "is there REALLY no coming back from this? Is he really dying? Is there not some hope?"

"I'm very sorry," he said, "but no, there is no coming back. He is basically gone; the machines are keeping him breathing and his heart beating until you're all able to make the necessary decisions."

So, we really have to do this. No one was going to wake me up and tell me that this had all just been a really bad nightmare. Okay, I thought, try to collect yourself. Obie would want me to be strong through all of this. So, it was back to trying to make the decision about organ donation. Sadly, it became a very heated conversation. Emotions were high for all of us, but ultimately, we decided against donating. I know there are many, many people that will be upset when reading this, but without being in our shoes, you can't know. I was upset myself! You can't know how hard it was to decide. Bottom line, after back-and-forth discussions, and talking with the doctors, it was decided because of all the trauma, medications and duration of time that Obie had fought for his life, it was questionable whether or not his organs would be worthy. And with all he had already been through, we couldn't bear the thought of making him suffer through anything more. Sounds crazy, perhaps. You can't know unless you are faced with this decision and everyone's circumstances are different. Does it haunt me? YES, because Obie's wishes were to donate. I hope that he can forgive us. I hope that everyone can forgive us. It haunts me to this day.

The amazing nurses delivered our decision to the harvesters. I couldn't do it. I couldn't face them. JJ was there with us. She was also amazing. She would not leave my side. She told me she would not leave me alone; she would not leave until Chad got there. No one could have removed me from my son's room. It was not happening! JJ stayed with me throughout the night. We took turns talking to Obie, holding his hand, singing to him. I just tried to absorb every part of him. He was leaving us, and I would never see my son again. My beautiful son was dying. I don't know when the 16th turned into the 17th; it all just ran together. Chad was not able to get there until late night on the 17th. We were keeping Obie alive so that he could say good-bye. Chad and I stayed with him again that night. I COULD NOT leave him. So, the next morning would be it. December 18, 2013 would be the day that my son left us. Could it really be happening? PLEASE, someone just wake me up!

December 18, 2013 ~ *My Angel, My Son 11:34 A.M.*

Nurse K was so comforting. I can't imagine how hard this type of care and work is for such people. She kicked everyone out of Obie's room so that she and I could prepare him to die. I still can't grasp all of this. She told everyone that this was precious time only for the mother. She reminded me that I had brought my son into this world, it was only right that I was able to prepare him to leave. It was very compassionate of her; I was very grateful. It was so very difficult, but I was grateful. We bathed him and combed his beard. We couldn't comb or wash his hair because of all the incisions and bleeding. We sang some of his favorite songs, some of the lullaby's that I used to sing to him when he was little, when I would put him down for a nap, or for the night. We sang the "Brahms's Lullaby" that he loved, especially on the music box. "You Are My Sun Shine" and others. I applied some of the oils that I had gotten for him, Frankincense and Helichrysum. We played Christmas music, of course. When we were done, she hugged me, told me how very sorry she was and then she had to leave. Another nurse would take over to prepare Obie to be removed from the machines. This was Nurse S (he was very kind as well). Everyone was allowed back into the room. It was filled with people. Myself, Obie's dad and stepmom, Chad (my Chad), JJ, Chad H, the Captain from his ship, SC from his ship, Chaplain G, and others.

So, this was it. It was time.

Obie's dad asked the nurse to please remove the hospital bands, which he did and then he began to remove the tubes, wires, and equipment. He asked all of us to please leave the room while they took my son off the ventilator. He said that it was a very unpleasant experience and told us that we probably did not want to be present. We took his advice. Once the ventilator was removed, we were all allowed back in. The room became very quiet, very still, other than Christmas music and the sounds of despair and heartache. We had placed all of the Christmas decorations at the head of Obie's bed. Chaplain G allowed Obie's dad and I to help anoint him with blessed oils and we all said a prayer for him. I wanted to get up in the bed and hold him, like I used to hold him when he was young and needed comforting, but there was not enough room and I was afraid if I bumped him in any way I'd make the bleeding worse. I was lost. I didn't know what to do! I could hold his hand. I could touch his arms, softly stroke his brow and the beard he had always wanted to grow. But I was afraid to hold him. It haunts me to this day! He just had to lie there by himself, with all of those people watching him die.

And then time stood still once more. It's not something that I can explain other than to say it felt like utter despair and torture. At the same time it wasn't real, or at least it shouldn't have been. To have to just stand there and wait. At some point, I whispered into Obie's ear how very much I loved him, how incredibly proud I was of him since the day he was born, and that it now was time for him to Soar with the Eagles. I don't know how much time passed, but I felt him go and I asked the nurse, he checked and my son's heart had stopped beating. He was gone. His heart beat for the last time at 11:34 A.M. on December 18th, 2013. Nurse S. no more announced his passing than his favorite Christmas carol, The Little Drummer Boy, started playing. Then the room lit up with bright light. It had been the grayest, dark rainy morning, but as the nurse pronounced Obie dead, the room filled with the brightest light. It was so bright that it made us all turn to look. Gazing out the window, we saw an opening in the gray sky and the shape of an angel with outstretched wings, omitting the light shining into the room. Obie was gone. His angels had come to get him. It wasn't a dream.

Once again, I don't know how long it took, but people began to leave the room. Nurse S told all of us that it would be some time before anyone would be able to come and get Obie's body. Finally, the only ones left in the room were Obie's dad, stepmom, Chad and myself. Then his dad and stepmom started to leave, yet Chad and I were still standing by his side. I wasn't leaving! I couldn't! I would not leave him by himself!

Obie's dad turned around and said to me, "he's dead you know, you can't bring him back." Of course, I knew that, but I was not going to leave him lying there by himself. Call me weird, call me crazy. I know everyone else thought that I was, but I didn't care. I would not leave him there alone. I asked Nurse S if I could please stay with him until they came to get his body. I told him that I could not watch them put my son into the bag, and asked him if he could please warn me when they arrived with the gurney, but please let me stay with him as long as I could. He allowed us to stay. Chad (my Chad and Bless him) stayed with me. I think it was about 45 minutes before they came. I cannot begin to tell you how hard it was to walk away – Cannot begin to tell you! He fought for his life for 38 days and now he's gone.

As we were walking away, one of the nurses that had cared for him (she was wonderful) called out my name. She'd heard what had happened. I turned around. She ran up to me and held me for a moment and said how very sorry she was. She was crying. Chad and I somehow made it to our hotel room and nothing seemed real. This could not be real!

PART 3

Forever in Ashes

YOU CAME HOME

Sometimes the darkness and emptiness is more than we
can bear / A darkness and emptiness that only a mother
can know / But, we try to find the light, For Our Children
*   – "For Our Children," by Laurie Powell*

T
HE COAST GUARD TOOK OVER THE ARRANGEMENTS for Obie's cremation, for
which we were grateful. The Coast Guard did try so hard. We had the option of
having him buried at Arlington Cemetery, but we thought that he would rather
come home. His dad and I picked out a beautiful Urn that has a pewter Eagle with its
wings outstretched and wrapped around it; they had it rush shipped. I didn't want to
leave Seattle without my son's ashes. Chad H and FE continued to be there for us, as
well as JJ. Chad and I didn't book our flight home immediately because we were
waiting to hear when we could take Trav home.

JJ asked what we would want to do while we were waiting. The first thing I wanted
to do was walk down to the pier and have a talk with Mother Ocean. I had some words
that I needed to say. We did that and I had my talk, I spoke my mind. Chad and JJ were
gracious to allow me the space and time to do that. While there we continued to wander
aimlessly around the Waterfront Pier and I happened to look inside a little shop that
had a blown glass Christmas Tree. I was immediately drawn to it, of course. It
reminded me of my son, my Angel. I asked the shop owner if I could purchase one.
She asked for some reason why I wanted to buy it. I told her that Christmas was my
son's favorite time of year and that he had just passed away the day before.

She started to cry and said, "you know, he is here with you right now, I can feel
him, he has such a strong presence." She then showed me the gooseflesh on her arms
and said that she had never had that happen before. I purchased the tree, we hugged
and then Chad, JJ and I made our way down the boardwalk. I heard someone saying
"hey lady, hey lady"; we all turned around and it was the shop owner running after
us. She had a stone in her hand and she told me that she wanted me to have it. She
put it in my hand, held it for a moment, hugged me again and left. I looked at the

stone. The word GRACEFUL was engraved into it, in Asian writing. What a wonderful gesture from a complete stranger. I was so touched. I still have it.

We then went on to one of JJ's favorite stores that showcased artisans from all over the world. We walked in and started wandering throughout the store. There were so many beautiful things made by such talented artists. I walked past a case and then took a couple of steps back and looked again. A very small ring had caught my eye. The young lady behind the counter asked if I had found something that I would like to look at. No, I told her, but I had just noticed the ring inside the case and thought it was beautiful. She brought it out and asked if I would like to try it on. Once again, I told her no, there's no way that it would fit and we wouldn't be able to afford it anyway. I ended up giving in to her persuasion and it was a perfect fit. The ring was Rose Gold with the tiniest little diamonds embedded all the way around it. The artist had named it Eternity. Diamond was Obie's birthstone and he is forever in eternity, "endless life after death." Yes, once again we all shed tears and she spoke to her supervisor about a price decrease. It's a ring I never take off.

I'm so grateful to JJ for her time with us, her time with me. Staying by my side until Chad was able to arrive; I'm grateful for all of her visits at the hospital and the time she was able to spend with Obie and his dad, for the time she spent with us after Obie's passing trying to keep our minds occupied. It couldn't have been easy. It was a great loss for her as well. A great loss for all!

The Urn arrived, but the cremation could not be scheduled in time for us to take Obie home with us. We had to leave Seattle without him.

Once again, I have no words, I cannot explain my grief.

On our flight home, it did not get any better. I don't remember exactly what happened but our flight from Seattle arrived in Salt Lake late and our connecting flight to Idaho Falls had already left. The deserted airport created a horrible feeling, intensifying how I already felt. Even though we missed our connection, our luggage made it. An airline employee offered an overnight kit (toothbrush/toothpaste/comb) with minimal empathy. We got on the phone and found a taxi to take us to a hotel for the night. It was well past midnight, dark and still.

My oldest sister and brother-in-law met with us the following morning before our flight home. I'm not sure when we finally made it to Idaho Falls, but our family members were there to meet us at the gate. Many hugs, many tears. I can't explain it, I felt as if I were a robot. I was there, yet I wasn't there. I was moving, but I wasn't sure how.

Chad and I finally made our way to the house, an hour away from Idaho Falls. Family and friends had strung some Christmas lights around the deck railing for us and even put up a Christmas Tree in the house. The gestures were beautiful and their thoughtfulness was so appreciated, we loved it. Everyone was wonderful and had done so much to help us, to try to help us through it all.

Now home alone, in the dim quiet, just Chad and I, a feeling overtook me, a memory-thought that'd been interweaved into this nightmare since November. Looking out the window I saw the amber-twinkle lights that I had not finished stringing on the trees back before everything. The world would change as I strung those lights. Now they are still there, unfinished, frozen in ice and snow.

SC brought Obie home on December 23rd. He made it home for Christmas after all. He hadn't been home for Christmas since he'd gone into the Coast Guard nine years earlier and now he was home. He was in ashes, forever in ashes, but he made it home. Obie's family, friends, the Honor Guard and citizens of Idaho Falls were all there to welcome my son home and pay their respects. I am so grateful to all of those that took the time and made the effort to come that day. It was a beautiful tribute to a young man who was so very, very loved. Our Hero. My beautiful son, forever in ashes.

SONS ARE THE ANCHORS OF A MOTHER'S LIFE ~ SOPHOCLES

My son was my life – my anchor. There is a big empty space, a huge void, since the day that Obie passed, and I've been cast adrift. A part of me died and went with him that day. I know, sadly, these are the feelings of too many parents. As a parent, you are lost.

I have been told by many that "*HIS PASSING WAS A BLESSING.*" He never would have wanted to live in the body that he would have been left with. I believe that in one respect, and I would never have wanted him to suffer, even if it meant him staying with us. In another respect, I struggle. I saw how hard he fought; I saw what he accomplished. He fought against all odds. None of the doctors thought he would live through the first night. He not only lived through the night, he stunned and amazed all of them. He accomplished things that he should not have been able to do, given his injuries and his condition. But he was strong. Strong in mind, will and spirit. He was our VIKING WARRIOR.

He was so determined and had such a strong will, no one can truly say what life would have been like for him. I can't help but think that he would have continued to do amazing things, as we already saw him do. But, no one can say that for sure. We don't have the answers and, it's not up to us in the big scheme of things. In fact, when he passed, I could feel how confused he was because he fought so hard to live. One last surgery and we were on our way to Palo Alto, and he knew this.

It haunted me after we came back home, so I finally went to see a Shaman to have her help him transition. I'm glad that I did, and I am very grateful to her for helping him find some peace with what happened. I know, I know. Some of you are calling me crazy again, and that's okay, I can take it.

I've always tried to live by the belief that one should make the most of each day and every moment. Spend as much time as possible with those you love and never miss the opportunity to tell them that you love them – always tell them that you love them. Don't miss those moments. Don't take your time with people for granted. Don't have regrets because you don't always get do-overs. Be grateful for every single day that you have with them.

IT DIDN'T ADD UP

The Search / Anger

F/V ALASKA Mist anchored and holding 8.5 NM from the closest point of land. F/V PAVLOF enroute with 0930L ETA. Intent of PAVLOF is O/S presence in case anchor doesn't hold. RESOLVE coordinating to have helicopter with diver o/s to un-foul screw with midday ETR. WAESCHE's H65 being repositioned from D/H (Dutch Harbor) to CB (Cold Bay). CB H60 on alert and is approximately 30 NM from distress scene. F/V ALASKA MIST identifying non-essential personnel, but plan to leave on ship unless situation worsens. Weather forecast to improve throughout the day and remainder of the week.

- Nov 11, 2013 Email from Incident Management to Waesche/Captain

M Y STRUGGLE WITH ALL OF THIS IS THE FACT that none of this ever should have happened in the first place. Obie never should have been placed in the front of the small boat; no one should have. It starts with Coast Guard Headquarters allowing the equipment to remain faulty from the beginning. What happened to the "formal request," to have the SRP retrieval equipment fixed, that had been placed four years prior to Obie's death? Was it shuffled, was it filed? Why was it "not a priority?" Was it because it would have taken the Waesche out of commission for the time that it would have taken to have all of the malfunctioning equipment fixed? It might have affected the Congressional funding for the upcoming ships, but it was okay for my son to die? Only then did it become "a priority." Had the equipment been fixed then someone wouldn't have been placed in the front of the small craft. It starts at the top and trickles all the way down the chain, to the command of the ship. All of these problems started from the time that the Deepwater Program was put in place. Google that if you have some time. It goes quite deep, no pun intended. I say God Bless and thank you to those that had the guts and integrity to stand up for what was right and make known what was going amiss in the beginning stages of the Deepwater Program. But the Coast Guard Headquarters still didn't pay attention, and they took ownership of ships that didn't operate properly and hold up at sea. They had malfunctioning equipment and the Headquarters always knew it.

But this isn't just about a malfunctioning piece of equipment, or the command's failure to rectify that issue. This is a multi-layered situation that resulted in the death of my son. There are numerous factors at play here. The Waesche had no good reason to remove the fishermen from the Alaska Mist when and how they did. Some may disagree, and that's alright. We all have our views and interpretations, as was proved by how the Coast Guard presented "The Accident." But my focus here, is to present different sides to the story.

This is my interpretation, along with the interpretation of many that were involved and many that were not. Interpretations from Coast Guard personnel through all the ranks – retired, veteran and active. Those that have a different view, I suspect, are the ones that remain quiet. Some were frightened: to speak the truth could result in the end of their careers. I understand this and would never want that to happen. I honestly can't think of anything more they can do or take from us. What more can someone take, beyond the life of a loved one?

Some of Obie's shipmates totally changed their stories from what they had been telling me in the beginning. For six years they were telling me how it never should have happened, that what happened on that day was wrong, and the reasons behind it were wrong too. During the creation of this book, one person flipped his story and went to the extent of saying "We were excited; we thought of it as a mini-vacation of sorts, going aboard a fishing boat." The emotions that flood through me are challenging. There must be good justifications for the things good people do. I am angry and frustrated, but I am also concerned for the well-being of my son's shipmates and his friends, the best of friends. I just want the truth, and it pains me that it's so hard to get at.

What would be the motive for Coast Guardsmen to change their stories? Is this some form of grieving – Bargaining? Along the way I found that it was not just some people who changed their stories to me, but also the Coast Guard Investigative Report itself was full of changed testimony – that is, the Coast Guard manipulated the testimony of the crew of the Waesche. Many people had many stories, and many of them did not add up. Careers are on the line. And family men need careers.

My eternal gratitude goes to those who loved my son, period.

* * *

A S MENTIONED, THE FAULTS ARE LAYERED and the story is not linear, not in a chronological way anyhow. We can take this back to Coast Guard culture at the turn of the century if we wanted to. Though, maybe the most useful starting point is with the National Security Cutters themselves. As this was a publicity stunt that ended poorly – even if it was a publicity stunt for one man.

The Deepwater Program is the post 9/11 congressionally approved plan for modernizing the Coast guard fleet. Specifically, the old High Endurance Cutters which were built in the early stages of the War on Drugs. The Deepwater Program was worth billions of dollars, and those who could pitch their ideas successfully, normally had some personal benefit. This resulted in less-than-optimal results. The new fleet of cutters, especially the first round of National Security Cutters were faulty to say the least. The information on this is a google click away, there are many to choose from. A very interesting article is: GAO January 16, GAO-16-148, National Security Cutter. That accessories and auxiliary equipment wouldn't work. Etc.... Some of the problems we've learned well in my son's story.

Some equipment, though it was malfunctioning, was pushed into service anyway. The prime example is the complete catastrophe of the stern launch ramps for the small boat. On Obie's ship, multiple pieces of equipment for this one process were known to malfunction. Instead of fixing the equipment, they used the crew as jerry-rigs. This is the same thing the Russians did in the Great Wars – march their troops ahead of the tanks in mine fields, to protect the tanks.

It is more than just equipment: Ego and advancement played a huge role. All parties that were involved with this incident were up for or hoping for promotions. From the District Commander/Vice Commandant who was also the Convening Authority over the Investigation, to the Captain and all the way down the chain of command. Completing a specific objective, like a SAR, has personal rewards. For the crew it means good conduct medals or mission medals. For the officers it is a check mark on their advancement papers. For the Coast Guard, it's automatic publicity, especially when the Deadliest Catch is over your shoulder. The incentive structure forces competition and unnecessary risk taking throughout the guard – and often the machinery fails because of it, and the crew is left to pick up the slack.

Public Image: They had to portray this as an "urgent, life threatening" SAR because that was the only way that they could save face after what happened that day. They had to maintain the public image of the United States Coast Guard. If moving the crew off of the Alaska Mist was necessary for safety, why did the helicopters wait for the cameras of the Deadliest Catch before retrieving the crew? Not to mention waiting until the next morning. Can the Coast Guard explain the benefit of having an Entertainment Company's filming equipment onboard a small helicopter during a life-threatening evacuation?

Crew have stated that they were told they had to "get the numbers up." Every operational Coastie will tell you that they are ordered to produce results. This means that the mission is not just about deterring or assisting, it means that the creative process must go into mission finding. If the NSC's didn't prove themselves, the Coast Guard would be in trouble with Congressional funding. They had to "GET THE NUMBERS."

There was also a toxic mix of Command present, according to emails I have. Not all of them were bad. There were good people in the chain of command, thank God for them. As in all things, there is the good with the bad. But the bad, made it dangerously bad! There was a total lack of regard and respect for the crew. They felt like numbers, not humans. Some had lost their sense of who they were. They felt expendable and some had lost a sense of who they were. They were overloaded in terms of work and stress. They could never catch their breath. They were sleep-deprived because of constant drills at all times of day and night. They nicknamed the captain "Captain Cowboy" because he couldn't be reined in. This wasn't a term of endearment by any means. This wasn't a nickname to be proud of.

* * *

I WILL NEVER BE OK WITH WHAT HAPPENED TO MY SON. There is no peace for me in this story, because the position and environment he was placed in, was not acceptable. Obie operated under the assumption that his command was operating in good faith. He assumed that his command would allow his shipmates to do their duty – like shutting the rear doors; like tagging-out the stern launch; like ensuring the best operator is in control on the bridge during risky operations. Obie was led to believe he was with professionals acting for the benefit of others. He did not know they were acting for their own purpose, with no merit, and with no values: Honor, Respect, or Devotion.

Is Obie a hero? Yes! He becomes even more heroic when one considers the circumstances he faced that day. He knew the terrible risks they were taking and yet he volunteered. "Someone is going to get hurt on this one." Those were the last words he was heard to say before he got into the small craft. He would rather it have been him than someone else. He took it for the team. That is the definite quality of a hero.

"Greater love as no man than this: To lay down one's life for one's friends."
– John 15:13

SHIPMATES AND STORIES

After the incident, they put the totalled SRP in the yard and didn't even have the decency to cover it up. We all had to walk past it, day in and day out, and look at it.

—Obie's Shipmate

MY SON'S FRIENDS AND SHIPMATES flooded into my life. As soon as they could, they reached out to me, and became as close as family. We visited. We shared stories.

Over the years, many of us became intertwined with the accounts of that day and stories of Obie, their memories. We craved the truth and we craved answers from the command.

Below are the authentic and unedited experiences of two of these men. I am choosing to keep their names for myself, though some of you may know who they are. I wish them both peace with this and I wish them both the world.

SHIPMATE AND FRIEND

It was November 2016, 3 years after we loaded an injured Obie into a helicopter in the middle of the Bering Sea. I sat at the airport bar in Salt Lake City talking to a guy who had been an MP in the army for a few years, gone down range for a couple of tours and was trying to get his shit together. We talked together, but in my mind I was still thinking about what I was going to say to Obie's parents. A lot went on that day of the accident and I didn't fully process it all until the investigation and began exploring how and why we'd wound up in that situation. My mind ran through the events of that day over and over, and my cop sensibility kept prodding me to consider what types of questions the investigators might ask and how I should answer them. I realized I had more questions than answers.

I was curious about everything happening in the aftermath of the accident. I wanted to know what had gone on in Obie's past. We had all been praying for the Obie and the family, but we were pretty much in the dark about what was actually happening. Because of the time of year, flights were hard to line up. Many people were stranded at airports. As I rushed to board my plane, I felt my emotions surging. I was traveling to close out one of the biggest chapters in my life. I felt confused. In some way I wondered why I was taking this trip, yet I also knew I had to. Boarding, I texted Tracey to let her know I was on my way. She texted back a 'love you' and 'safe flight'. As I always do when I fly, I let the flight attendant know I'm a medic. 'Thanks! Hope we won't need you," she said. I smiled and agreed.

As I stepped off the plane in Idaho I was excited to close one chapter in my life and open another. Seeing Laurie and Chad as I passed the security zone, my heart beat faster and my emotions soared as I gave them big hugs. We had all been through three years of hope and anxiety. I had ten thousand questions for them and I think I tried to get them all in before we went to the restaurant.

Later, we walked into the restaurant and Laurie explained that Obie had pretty much grown up there. I looked around and could see it. The aroma of food from the kitchen was amazing as we ordered wine, looked at the menu and talked about the restaurant. Having lived in Alaska and Seattle, I considered myself an excellent judge of seafood and the fish we had that night was some of the best ever. On my way to the bathroom, I tried to catch Obie's dad for a second, but he was manning the door and we didn't really get a chance to talk. We did talk about fishing a little, and I managed to show him photos on my phone of fish I'd caught through the years.

On the drive to the house, I was amazed again. Having lived in cities for so many years, I'd forgotten what stars looked like and how peaceful the cold nights could be. Soon, because Laurie had promised snow, we loaded up and headed to Wyoming. Because it was off-season, only a few places were open for business, but I liked that a lot more than if we'd been sharing space with a lot of tourists. We walked around town and decided to grab a bite to eat at the Silver Dollar. It was a unique restaurant with western art on the walls and a bar top inlaid with silver dollars. I remember we ordered a Blue Moon (Obie's favorite beer) and sandwiches. This was a cool stop because we talked about the owl that had landed on the boat a few days before Obie got hurt.

We finished lunch and the bartender asked if we wanted to flip a silver dollar for our bill. He said if we guessed the correct flip, we would only have to pay for our beer and not the meal; if we guessed wrong, it would cost us an additional seventy-five cents. Laurie flipped first, called 'Heads' and boom, it was Heads. I flipped, saying 'Tails Never Fails' and boom—there it was. So, we paid for our two beers and left. We joked about it all the way back to the house.

Ever since I was a child, I held the date November 11th tight in my heart; now I held it tighter because it was also the day that Obie was critically injured. This day will always have added meaning for me and other crewmembers on board. As we walked to the memorial, a million things ran through my mind. We sat down and I felt the sun on my back.

"I miss my boy," Laurie said.

"I miss him, too," I said.

I went live on social media and I could see hundreds of people jump in, paying their respects. After an hour or so, we sat there talking about the finer things in life. Obie's dad jumped over the creek and invited us over to his restaurant. Laurie and I sat down to talk, but Obie's dad had to watch the door. I wanted him to come over and sit with us, but we all knew where the conversation would go and it was tough enough as it was. Later, we cruised back to the house and started a fire in the fire pit.

...

It was December 18th, 2014, exactly one year after Obie passed away. It wasn't the day he left the ship, but the day he drew his last breath. We were underway on a mission when they announced a special quarters for all hands on the flight deck. As I climbed up the ladder, I saw Senior Chief in his tropical dress uniform standing next to a wreath with some of the nicest flowers I'd ever seen in my life. I wondered how they'd been kept so nice. While these boats are underway, it's hard to keep lettuce nice, let alone flowers. Directly across from Senior Chief was Boatswains Mate Second Class.

The new skipper/Captain, was moved and sorrowful as he spoke about Obie. He noted that he was speaking as if he'd known him, and he wished he had given the legacy Obie left behind aboard the Waesche. As tears fell and shipmates mourned, Senior Chief and BM2 slowly brought the wreathe to the stern of the boat and tossed it into the water. Just before it hit, the wreath spun, causing a lot of the flowers to scatter. Later, talking to BM2, we agreed that Obie flipped it to make us laugh.

The night before, all the people that were there when the incident occurred met behind the pilot house to say a prayer for Obie and his family. It was pretty cool. We sang Amazing Grace and shared stories about Obie that had everyone laughing. Eventually, though, the crowd slowly broke up and everybody went about their night.

Throughout the year I didn't say much about what happened and tried to avoid thinking about it too much. Yet, I'd wake up every morning with thoughts of Obie and the accident running through my mind. At every meal, I'd try to sit at a table that was farthest away from the Battle Dress Station table, and I'd sit with my back to it. On most Coast Guard boats the mess deck is where the Battle Dress Station is located. That is where the wounded are taken and treated, and that's why you take your hat off when transiting through, to pay your respects to the shipmates that have died on the mess deck. There is usually one table closest to the wall under high-powered lights shining down for surgeries. Next to the table is a large cabinet with medical supplies, oxygen, blankets and other equipment needed to treat medical casualties. Nowadays, the only time I get close to this table is when I'm conducting law enforcement training or medical training. Other than that, I hate looking at it or even walking past it.

…

My buddy from the Coast Guard cutter Stratton texted, asking me to come by because, he said, he had something for me. As I walked across the bow of the boat onto the flight deck, I saw a huge banner with the name OBENDORF with a huge American flag draped downward just like the ones from the famous pictures from 9/11. I felt a chill up and down my spine and I was proud to see the flag and the dedication from a sister ship. My buddy tossed a tee shirt to me and I saw on the back that it read Counter Narcotics. There were also three names listed: Obendorf, Horne and Bruckenthal. Senior Chief Horne was killed December 2nd, 2012 during pursuit of a drug-filled panga off the coast of Los Angeles near the Channel Islands. Bruckenthal was killed April 24th, 2004 alongside two U.S. Navy sailors while intercepting a waterborne suicide attack on an offshore oil terminal near the coast of Iraq in the Persian Gulf. I held that shirt up, saying man, it's awesome, a shirt full of Coast Guard heroes. My buddy said he'd saved it for me, and one with the names of all of our pursuit teams. I was excited and thankful.

…

On November 3rd I was typing up a statement for a law enforcement boarding from the day before. One of the Operational Specialists called down to my room and told me to switch the television to Channel 3, which was one of our security cameras. I did so and observed a brown and white owl perched on one of the safety cables on the bow of the boat. Its feathers were ruffled to stay warm and I could see one or two flip up on his back as the wind shifted. All of my shipmates in the birthing area were glued to the screen as the owl quickly shifted his focus. It looked as if the owl were peering through the camera into our room.

ET1 said, "Man, that is creepy. I'm going to take a picture of it."

Once it looked away, I quickly ran up to see from the bridge where people were also taking pictures. AG1, our TDY Navy weather specialist whose primary mission on the boat was to get us up to date information due to the fast-changing weather in the Bering Sea, responded to my asking her how it was going, "This is not good!"

"How do you mean?"

"It's a bad sign," she said.

Everyone looked around. Some looked worried; others looked like they thought she was crazy or superstitious.

"In my culture, if you see an owl in the daytime, it means death," she added.

"Are you serious?" I asked. She nodded her head yes. I walked out and went down to my room. MK2 walked in and I told him what the AG1 had said. He thought it sounded wild. I sat down at my computer and looked it up online. There were a lot of superstitions and myths about the owl from cultures all over the world, and the majority of them confirmed that death or ill will were evident. The more we talked, the more we wondered why this owl would be way out in the Aleutians and why would it land on our boat in the middle of the day.

Studies show and scientists believe there are approximately two hundred owl species. They are found in all regions of earth except Antarctica. It is believed in certain cultures that owls are associated with sorcery or evil. The Aztecs and Mayans believed that the owl was a symbol of death and destruction; the Aztec God of Death, Mictlantecuhtli, was often depicted with owls. In the native Cherokee culture, owls can be a bad omen. It is said that if you are outside in broad daylight and an owl flies over your head, a family member or loved one will die within the coming week. The scuttlebutt about the owl carried on for days; some treated it like a joke while others wondered if something bad was about to happen.

I was on the fantail talking to the EO when I observed the small boat approach the notch. I headed for HSC's office to help him with the medical questionnaires for the fishermen from the Alaska Mist when they arrived. As I was about thirty feet in the skin of the ship, I heard yelling and screaming coming from the fantail. I ran to the back deck and observed the small boat being slammed by the waves against the net. The boat was tossed against the net several times. I observed MK3 and the Coxswain assisting BM3 Obendorf by attempting to hold him up. There was a lot of blood leaking from his goggles down onto his face and dry-suit. He appeared to be unconscious.

Immediately I donned a PFD and yelled to BMC for permission to enter the boat area to assist in evacuating BM3 Obendorf from the small boat. When the stern doors closed, I assisted in retrieving him from the boat and moving him to the boat deck. I traversed the boat deck to start my assessment and evaluate the damage. I asked HSC to have the team get BDS set up and advised him we needed a stretcher for immediate transport. I observed a large amount of blood coming from Obie's mouth and facial area. There was extreme swelling in the maxilla area, and brain matter and blood were coming from his ears. I could hear a gurgling sound, leading me to believe that Obie was breathing but that fluids had partially blocked his airway. I used my fingers to spread his lips back and observe the inside of his mouth to determine where the blood was coming from. All of his teeth appeared to be in place and there were a few strings of skin tissue and a lot of blood.

While on the boat deck, I grabbed the stretcher and placed it on the righthand side of BM3 Obendorf, then asked a shipmate to hold cervical spine control. I advised the others that we were going to log roll Obie onto his left side to place him in the stretcher. We rolled him on the shipmates' count. I positioned Obie to keep his airway open and directed everyone to transport him to BDS. I checked his airway again and suctioned a lot of fluids from his mouth with manual hand suction. GMC immediately took C-spine control. I asked the team to remove all clothing and expose all of the skin to see if there were further injuries and to gauge proper depths of the breathing. This would also allow us to take a better pulse reading.

I positioned myself on the side of BM3 Obendorf so I could provide immediate care. Upon exposure, I took his pulse bilaterally and could feel that it was weak on both wrists. His pupils were equal and dilated but not reactive to light. I advised FS2 to raise Obie in the shock position and I started the primary survey. I asked Obie several times if he could hear me and I did not get a response. I then asked him to squeeze my hand if he could hear me and he responded with his right hand. I told him he would be ok and that I was going to take care of him; he squeezed my hand two times. I asked for a pulse/oxygen meter and a set of vital signs. I asked GM2 to record all of the events as they happened. I detected ausculator sounds in both lungs and there did not appear to be any signs of rhonci or rales in the lungs. I told Obie I was going to check him to see if he had any other injuries and he squeezed my hand as if agreeing with me. I asked him to squeeze my hand if he felt any pain while I was checking him. FS2 then began squeezing Obie's left leg to check for deformities, contusions, abrasions, penetrations, burns, lacerations and swelling (DCAPBLS). Then he moved over to Obie's right leg. I asked Obie if he could feel that and he squeezed my hand. I asked if it hurt and he did not squeeze. When we arrived at the pelvis Obie did squeeze my hand and I noted the discomfort and so advised HSC.

ENS palpated the stomach for rigidity and distinction and had negative results; he then moved to the chest and also had negative results. I did not feel Obie squeeze my hand during the rest of the pain and injury assessment. I advised the team that we were going to roll him onto his right side to look for DCAPBLS and to remove the dry suit and other clothing from under him. We moved on GMC's count. No further injuries were found and I asked if there was any fluid loss around the rectum; none was noted or observed. I ausculated lung sounds on his back and found them clear on the top and bottom of his lungs with no signs of rhonchi or rales. I then asked FS3 to take Obie's hand to continue communication with him and to let him know he could still communicate if he needed anything.

We rolled Obie onto his back and I requested several blankets to keep him warm. We covered him up and raised his feet (shock position), then I asked FS3 to grab some 4X4 gauze to cover and wrap Obie's hand laceration. The laceration was not bleeding and was on the top of his right hand. I advised BM3 that we were going to place a cervical spine collar on Obie and that it was going to be a little uncomfortable. Obie's respirations appeared to be getting shallower and his oxygen level started to drop. I asked GM2 to set up oxygen on a non-re-breather. I suctioned Obie's airway again and administered the oxygen. Minutes later, Obie made a sound like he was going to be sick and I rolled him on his left side as he projectile-vomited what appeared to be a quart of blood and food on the floor. I suctioned his mouth and assured him that I was going to take care of him and stay strong for us. I placed him on his back and asked for another set of vital signs. I placed the re-breather back on him and osculated lung sounds again. The lung sounds still appeared to be clear. I asked for the AED and advanced airways in case the situation worsened. They laid them to my left at the top of Obie's head. I told Obie I was going to begin cleaning his face to look good for the nurses in Anchorage and he squeezed my hand tightly.

Due to the severe blood loss, I asked HSC to grab Obie's medical records to see what blood type he was and gather any information on allergies or medications (blood thinners, etc.). I asked Obie to squeeze my hand when I went down the line to see what blood type he was. I started with A, proceeded to B, then to O with no response. I asked Obie if he could still hear me and he responded, squeezing FS3's hand. I asked him if he did not know his blood type and he squeezed her hand again. HSC returned and reported that he could not find the medical records. I asked Obie if the records were in his room and he squeezed FS3's hand; I asked if they were in his locker and he squeezed again. I asked a SN to recover Obie's medical records from the locker.

HSC returned and advised us that the helicopter was fourteen minutes out and we started an IV in Obie's right arm. I asked them to splint around it to keep Obie from bending it and breaking the catheter. I removed the re-breather to suction the inside of his mouth and then replaced it. I took vital signs again and advised Obie that he was going to be ok, the helicopter was on its way. I requested a clear path to the flight deck hanger through the outside of the ship to allow four personnel to carry the litter. I asked FS3 to carry the IV and to lay it on Obie while going up the ladder.

We arrived at the hanger and Obie made a sound as if he were going to be sick again and squeezed my hand. I held C-spine and rolled him on his right side, but he did not vomit. I told him that the ride was ready and that we were going to get him better help. We re-secured him to the stokes litter and I told him to keep squeezing my hand, and that when he heard the first non-AFN commercial, he better think about me. He squeezed my hand really tight. I told him to hold onto the strap, keep counting to twenty and squeezing to keep his mind in the game. I checked his blood pressure, then his lung sounds to see if they were clear. I placed the oxygen between his legs and secured it under the strap and blanket. The crew then escorted him to the helicopter. I heard the blades turning and cutting through the cold air. I was adjusting the blankets on Obie to make sure he was comfortable and secure. I looked up for a second in the dim light of the hanger and saw a light of white eyes as the crew looked helpless with questions on their faces. I felt frozen. The facial expressions never changed.

The starboard hatch opened, the cool air rushed in and the sound of the blades suddenly grew louder. The flight medic entered and it felt good to see a familiar face. It was the same one that had been on board for the majority of the patrol. I reported Obie's vital signs and updated information. As I departed the hanger, pulling the rubber gloves off my hands, I glanced at the hallways. The crew was moving in slow motion, as if everyone was in a dream. I walked around the corner toward doc's office and saw the fishermen. They looked at me and said they were sorry.

I knocked on the door and HSC opened it. I walked in. We looked at each other and knew we had to talk about it, though neither of us wanted to sit down and begin. For some reason I flashed to a story about Obie. One night I saw him and he had a bruise on his hand. I asked him what happened and he told me some guys jumped him on his way back from downtown. As the story circulated, we embellished it, starting a rumor that he'd fought off a pack of Kodiak bears. I smiled inwardly remembering that story.

The next day, we had quarters and everyone showed up. It was crisp and the cold air pierced me. Everyone was still. The silence amazed me. You could hear an eagle miles away. The CO and the XO came out and wanted to give us an update on Obie.

...

I was on duty and I saw the Senior Chief pull up and walk across the brow carrying a garment bag. I looked at the GPOW and she had a blank look on her face. I asked her what was happening. She said there had been a lot of people calling for the XO. I saw GMC come across the brow followed by OPS with garment bags in their hands. One of the security watch standers came out. By the time they made it to their rooms the quarterdeck consisted of my whole watch section. We were sitting in a circle and no one said a word. Some of us stared at the floor. The security watch stander walked by and told us they were clearing out Obie's locker and putting his things in a sea bag. That was it. That was the event that no one wanted to hear—the moment when Obie's belongings were taken off the boat. By the next day, you could see the frustration of not knowing and the fear of the unknown in the crew's eyes.

I got off duty the next morning and drove home. All the way, I did not know what to say to my wife. I had to say something, but what was there to say? I still didn't know anything.

...

I stood there in my topical blues waiting for Mrs. Ong's class to finish lunch. I was excited to have something to do, anything to get my mind off all the thoughts that whirled in my brain. The sun shone and my uniform was crisp. I knew I had to make a great impression and I really wanted to get my mind off Obie. I walked into the classroom and saw all the kids staring at the shiny parts of my uniform. I could see the anticipation on their faces and the anxiety of having to wait to ask questions they'd prepared on yellow sticky notes.

I began with an introduction, telling them I served on a boat that did search and rescue, helicopter rescue and all of the fun stuff. Their questions were as I expected. One kid asked if we had Xbox on the boat. Yes, I explained, we actually had them linked to each other so we could play other crew all around the boat. Another student asked if we had ice cream aboard. Oh, yes, I answered, and the cooks always stock up on the best flavors, too. Towards the end of the period, a student asked "has anyone ever died on your boat?"

My body dropped, my knees felt week and I stood there wondering how best to answer. I remember staring at the back wall while an inner voice commanded "Say something!" Were they too young for the truth? Of course not! He'd asked the question. I wanted to speak, but at first, I couldn't say Obie's name. Just the thought of saying it made me tear up and my heart felt like it was racing a million beats per second. I looked at my wife, who stood at the back of the room, and she began talking about something else. I glanced at Mrs. Ong, who looked back at me with anxiety. I turned around to face the board and silently told myself to get my shit together. I turned back around and launched back into the demonstration as if the question had never been asked. I went on for five more minutes, but the question came up again. I told myself, this is happening and you're going to finish this. I asked Mrs. Ong to look up Travis Obendorf on line. The photo popped right up. It was the one everyone on the ship remembers when they close their eyes. It was the first photo used by news media when the incident was reported. It showed Obie standing with his Coast Guard issued dry suit on. He looked relaxed, like he was hanging out. In the background was the Pacific Mariner, a crab fishing boat that was large enough to require a big boarding team. You could see how relaxed he appeared to be as he braced his left hand on the baton; he looked as if he were in the middle of a conversation, probably with OS3 or the SN. I remember the fishing boat crew that day was a little nervous because they didn't know what we were looking for. At the same time, they were happy to see another face other than the crew they saw every day. I think the boarding crew had similar feelings. I heard them cutting up, joking and laughing. I remember yelling at them to stop laughing, which made them laugh even harder. The crew had a large bin of candy on deck, and we asked them if they were expecting trick-or-treaters. Since it was only the 17th of October, it would be a wait. The fishermen laughed, explaining that the sugar gave them incentive to stay awake and haul in crab pots.

...

I was standing in line for coffee and heard the coastie in front of me as someone grabbed him in passing and said, "Hey, man, I thought you were stationed in Florida now."

"I am," the other said, "but I'm out here for Obie's memorial."

I realized I'd been in Bahrain with him. I was glad to see a lot of people come out to pay their respects.

...

I had just finished shining my shoes and putting my dress blouse on with my ribbons and awards when Senior Chief approached and asked if I had a minute. I did. He asked if I would help escort Obie's family around. I said I would be honored to do so. As I looked around the flight deck, I saw that the crew looked as if they were living through that day all over again. I could sense the tension in the air, but there was also anticipation to see Obie's family. There was so much people wanted to say. We all wanted to meet those who had made Obie the awesome friend and shipmate he had been. We stood silently as the family crossed the brow onto the boat and a lot of the crew had the balls of their feet dug in as if they wanted to sprint up to them and just surround them with the love we felt for Obie.

Obie's mom approached me and said, "Senior Chief told me you were one of the EMT's that helped him."

"Yes, Ma'am," I said. "Obie made it easy for me." I told her how I'd done everything I could and she thanked and told me how sorry she was that I'd had to go through that. I told her I was so happy to have the time we did with her son. From that moment on, I just wanted to know more and talk about everything Obie did. I wanted to get to know his family. The family spent a lot of time walking around and made time to talk to anybody that approached them.

The Senior Chief asked if everyone was ready to head over to the galley to eat. I was still talking to Obie's mom. She mentioned it was probably time to start moving and I escorted her to the galley. As we walked towards the pier, we saw one of the K9 vehicles and she asked if there was a puppy in there. I told her, yes, those were our bomb dogs. We used them during major events for security. She told me she missed her dogs back home and would give anything for a puppy kiss just then. I told her I could make it happen. As we walked slowly down at the back of the pack, I texted one of the dog handlers, my buddy Chris Hartman. I told him that Obie's mom would like to meet his dog; could he make that happen? Chris immediately shot back an answer that he was on his way. We met him outside the galley and introduced Obie's mom to Ebee. Laurie knelt down. Ebee bent his ears forward and started kissing her face. Laurie smiled from ear to ear and wrapped her arms around Ebee. After several seconds, Laurie stood up and looked like she'd inhaled a breath of fresh air.

"Thank you so much," she said to Chris. "That helped me so much!"

The Senior Chief came out and asked if we were ready. Laurie apologized right away, hoping I wasn't in trouble. The Senior Chief told her that the day belonged to her family and there was no way they could be late. I walked on with her to the memorial.

The sun was the highest it had been all day and the heat bore down on everyone as if Obie were saying he was happy we all showed up.

SHIPMATE AND FRIEND

The night of the incident was as powerful as the falling of the twin towers in my mind. I say that as it will forever be scarred in my head and I will forever remember it vividly.

I was a watch supervisor in CIC (Combat information Center) which is like the brain of the cutter, all operations and communications travel through CIC. I had just gotten off watch and knew that we had been planning to assist the F/V ALASKA MIST. The F/V had lost propulsion but still had power for heat/electricity. There were 22 fishermen onboard and from my recollection they were going to be assisted by commercial towing vessel until the towing vessel determined it to be too dangerous. That is when our Cutter started to head full speed toward the F/V ALASKA MIST to assist. We weren't even sure we would be the primary asset yet, but that didn't matter. This was normal for the WMSL crews, as the new ships were the shining stars of the fleet. They jumped at every situation and opportunity to show their capability.

The crew was constantly overworked/ and either training, conducting missions, or standing watch. The consensus was that the CG made an agreement with Congress to provide so many days out at sea, conducting the 11 missions, as part of an agreement to gain funding for additional WMSLs to be built. The idea was that we (Congress) will give you the cutters but you (USCG) need to justify the spending. This only got worse with sequestration and mismanagement of the plan for the WMSL program.

The original idea was that the Cutters would have two crews and a support unit to fill in any gaps. The crews were to be called Blue Crew and Gold Crew. There are many people in the CG today that still think this is happening. This design for personnel endurance was part of the agreement but was never upheld.

So the first WMSL was built, CGC BERTHOLF, complete with 113 crew members. They never made a second crew. The second WMSL, CGC WAESCHE, and the CGC STRATTON the third were built. Each with one crew, which is still how they operate today. The crews are called Crew ALPHA, Crew BRAVO, Crew CHARLIE, etc... depending on the numerical WMSL they are attached to. But crews were still obligated to be out at sea for the required amount of days in the agreement, I believe it was 210 days for the cutter to be deployed. The crew had a different endurance than the Cutter and was set to be out for 180 days before the swap would be needed. But the swap never occurred, because the second crews for each cutter never was formed. Instead the CG created the WMSL support building, a fancy building on CG Island in Alameda where a handful of people were stationed to "Support" the WMSLs. The majority of the people stationed there were crew that were deemed not fit for duty on the cutters. Reasons included pregnancy, medical, and mental issues and so on... this made going to sea not possible and they were moved temporarily to the WMSL Support unit. They used the support unit to hold "problem members" while they transitioned them out of the CG. In my view, this weakened the WMSL support system that much more.

The other issue was the three WMSLs all operated differently, so one may have a better rotation or be broke and unable to go to sea. This was critical as the WMSL support unit would allow its relief crew choice to work/support anyone of the three WMSLs. So obviously they would all go to the WMSL with the best rotation or the broken one to avoid going to sea. The CGC STRATTON, the third WMSL was broken so much it was referred to as "Building 752" mocking its hull number as a cutter. This was due to the other two WMSLs cannibalizing parts from it to keep operating. So the CGC STRATTON received most of the "support" as they never went anywhere and all they had to do is stand an in port watch on a rotation that was better than the other two WMSLs due to more people.

The CGC BERTHOLF made the first north patrol to the Bering Sea. The word that came back to the other WMSLs was the hull couldn't handle the climate and it was a huge failure testing the WMSLs in the Alaskan environment. The CGC BERTHOLF then was broken pier side along the CGC STRATTON. That left the CGC WAESCHE, during sequestration, which meant the other CG Cutters, 378s, 270s, and 210s that weren't broke from being old were told to not sail to save money. But the WMSL program needed to keep sailing as that little agreement to obligate X amount of operational days to keep building WMSLs needed to continue.

So the CGC WAESCHE was the only one left to sail, and it did. All the time. I felt like I was in the Navy I went out so much. Out for three months, in for two, then back out for four more, maybe in for one... constantly gone. At the same time you have CO's (Commanding Officers) competing with each other for accolades and awards in the race to make Admiral. The parent command of the CGC WAESCHE, PAC AREA, was constantly watching and tasking one thing after the next, but in between, the CO/ Command would task training and drills almost relentlessly. This was all thrown on the backs of the workhorses of the cutter, the crew. Focus on this and you begin to see the underlying problems that led to the tragic incident involving Obie.

To the casual observer, the situation may have looked like the mighty warship WAESCHE out doing the good deeds of the CG. But at what expense?

That was realized on the worse night of my career. Upon being relieved I was in a hurry to get back to my rack to get to sleep before my next watch. They were about to conduct the pre brief, a brief given in CIC where the CO and Operations Officer meet with the small boat crew/helo crew to discuss the mission, and concerns. I went to the door to leave and got stuck holding the door to let them all in CIC. Once they were in I thought I would hang out in the back and listen using the opportunity to monitor/critique my subordinates who were then on watch conducting the brief.

The case particulars were discussed and they got to weather and the Coxswain (the driver of the small boat) directly told the CO he didn't feel comfortable and it was unsafe. The Coxswain was then told if he didn't feel comfortable they would get another Coxswain to do it. The Coxswain then stated he could handle it and the brief continued.

Also during the brief, I saw one of my junior Petty Officers whispering something to the Senior Chief and pointing at his FLIR cameras on the stern of the cutter. The Senior Chief said something back to him and waved his hand like saying, I don't want to hear it. All this was wrong but similar to many operations onboard the WASCHE, where it became instruction over discussion. It was almost as if we were all numb to it. I left CIC as the brief finished up before the rush of the people attending it came barreling out the door. I went down to my rack and started to go to sleep. I just dozed off trying to ignore the pipes (announcements over PA system) while listening for important ones. It takes a while to learn to do that, but when you hear an important pipe, you jump. That is exactly what happened. The next thing I knew I hear; NOW BDS LAY TO THE MESSDECK. This is unusual as typically you hear "now corpsman" if a simple medical issue occurs, but BDS, is Battle Dressing Station which is typically made for major casualties and the need for a group of responders.

I jumped up, and threw on my pants and boots and run up to see if I can help. I climbed all the ladders, the boat is eerily quiet and nobody to be seen. I got to the mess deck and I start to hear commotion in the back so I head towards that area. When you walk in the mess deck you have to turn right and then left to head back to the stern. I was about to turn right and I ran right into the Coxswain, he was covered in blood and crying and in what looked like shock shaking his head and his eyes bulging out mumbling "help..." He did not look injured just mentally distraught. I went quickly farther back to see what's going on that caused this, I got to the long passageway that led back and people were carrying BM3 Obendorf in towards the mess deck. I grabbed ahold and helped carry him to the BDS table. One of the tables in the mess deck is fitted with giant medical lights and a triage cabinet to serve as a trauma center. At this point the HSC, Health Services Technician Chief and ME1, Maritime Enforcement First Class, who was a Corpsman in the Marines were getting ready to treat BM3. We lowered BM3 to the table.

He was in the worst medical condition I have ever seen, his eyes were rolling back, he had severe bleeding and what appeared to be clearish yellow spinal/brain fluid coming out of his left ear. He couldn't speak. I realized I was in the way and backed up slowly feeling the shock of trauma set in myself. It all happened very quickly but I have so much respect for ME1, The HSC was inevitably freaking out, panicky and seemed unsure of what to do. It's not every day you have a real medical incident and have to apply skills and training and I feel this may have been too much for HSC. ME1 however, I firmly believe kept BM3 alive and helped get him to the hospital in time. ME1 as I mentioned had experience from being overseas in the Army responding to actual battlefield trauma and medical emergencies. I stood staring at it all in disbelief and hope. I didn't even fathom the time that passed and then all of a sudden it was over.

I was standing in the mess deck alone, everyone had gone up to the flight deck and started to conduct the MEDEVAC of our shipmate. I stood for a moment and took in the environment and tried to process what had just happened. I looked over and the mess deck BDS table area and floor was covered in blood, the cabinet ripped apart, IVs sitting there, and I just immediately felt depressed and overwhelmed with sorrow. I thought what if everyone comes in and sees the same thing. So I quickly turned on the rest of the lights and the ETC (Electronic Technician Chief), saw me and asked what I was doing and I explained and he quickly started helping me. We got swabs (mops) from scullery, and we cleaned up all the mess and awaited hearing whether the helo made it to the tiny hospital. He would still have to be transferred to another hospital as we were in the middle of nowhere.

I am haunted almost every night of the images of seeing my buddy on that table helpless, of cleaning up his blood and thinking this should be in him and he should be here right now eating midrats (late night snack) with me on the mess deck. Why?... why did this happen? WHY WHY WHY! We finished cleaning, we both looked at each other and said nothing. I just went down to my berthing got back in my rack and laid there sleepless until watch. On watch is when I started questioning everything, the weather, who was OOD, what did the watch stander say to the Senior Chief? I was distraught as was the crew and we wanted answers, will he be ok? Why did this happen? I found out, the OOD was an ENS who had just got qualified. Also according to the Petty Officer on the radar who tried to talk to the Senior Chief, I later found out from him; He was saying the stern notch was taking in a lot of swells and it was unsafe. The Senior Chief told him the OOD will turn the boat if needed and mind your radar. "Mind your radar" is said to CIC watchstanders when you want them to go away or leave you alone and get back to doing their main job. So he basically brushed him aside and ignored his concerns.

The weather was horrible, we were not held on the proper bearing according to the weather log to recover the small boat. In the OODs defense I don't think even a seasoned OOD could have held position correctly in the variable swells and seas we were taking. The Coxswain was right during the initial pre brief, this was an unsafe and quite honestly an unnecessary operation. The F/V had power, we could have stood off and monitored them until weather cleared. There were SAR Helos ready in Kodiak, we didn't need to try to conduct passenger transfers in such unsafe conditions pressuring our Coxswains and ignoring their judgement. But we did.

We did it in my opinion to get that next big accolade, to complete another task first, to try to prove something. When it didn't work, we then stood down the transfer and towed them, but at the cost of one of our own. The best word to describe what happened is 'overzealousness'. Then the unspeakable occurred. They tried to cover it up.

Anyone involved were required to make a written statement, those statements were collected in the Wardroom. Different command personnel flew off to be with BM3 while at the hospital and to conduct meetings with family. The Mishap Analysis board (MAB) showed up, a group of random officers and subject matter experts to investigate. But prior to, the statements were not only screened by command, but abbreviated. The command took the statements and removed the ones that they didn't want presented to the MAB, the ones that were submitted (due to too much involvement to exclude completely) they abbreviated and took out anything that they didn't feel was necessary or implicating. My personal statement was removed from the final investigation. I know they changed others as I read many and also saw the final investigation given to BM3s parents years later. The statements the command submitted were not complete.

We were told we would meet his parents and they were flying out to the boat. Several of the crew onboard knew about how corrupt this situation was. Yet nobody said a word, not even me, for fear that it would absolutely shatter the parents, and some form of reprisal would be done to those who spoke out. This was due to things said to people onboard who got too vocal about the situation. The Petty Officer who was on the radar was literally removed from the CG for an unrelated incident a couple weeks later. I was treated unfairly in regards to my professional development and chastised for speaking out.

Too many coincidental and suspicious things followed that night. That is what got everyone talking, and after piecing it all together it's clear to see this could have been prevented and the command clearly protected itself. I know of many other situations regarding the Senior Chief and the family, but cannot speak to them personally, but they sound very accurate to the kind of heartless man the Senior Chief was.

The investigation regarding the misuse of the stern notch system was all factual and did lead to BM3s injuries. The design was wrong but the quick fix to put someone on the front and manually pull the catch line over was purely due to the drive to just keep working and get the job done. At the end of his tour, the CO was literally transferred to CG-751 (CUTTER FORCES) which was like a kick to the balls to everyone who knows how overzealous and unsafe his practices were. As of now he is not in the CG anymore I am not sure why, probably retired. The Senior Chief retired and got himself a cushy GS job in San Francisco controlling navigation of commercial traffic. The Operations Officer ended up advancing and working at PAC AREA, and then the XO of another cutter. The person in charge of PAC AREA at the time became the CG Commandant.

This event was the most sickening thing I have ever experienced. We (the crew) were told we would be given contact info for the parents to talk to them whenever we wanted, this information would be released by the command to the crew. This never happened, so we sat, we transferred, we moved on in our careers. We all still felt and feel bad about what happened and nobody dared say word. I felt my job and family's well-being would be at risk if I mentioned it. I was in fear, I still fear seeking mental help regarding not being able to remove the thoughts from my head. The images of that night, how unfair and completely opposite of what the CG stands for this was.

It wasn't until I got a call from ME1, that he couldn't take it anymore when he found Obie's mom online and reached out to her. I found out that she felt we all turned our backs on BM3 and his legacy; that we didn't care. She didn't realize nobody contacted her because we didn't know how and were subtly discouraged from doing so. ME1 found her and engaged the conversation. He discovered that she felt uneasy meeting us all that day on the boat and her motherly instincts told her something was wrong with what she was being told.

A conversation was had where the truth came out, about the many issues involving the investigation... She had already tried to get the Coast Guard to look into the investigation based on her hunches and the Commandant at the time (who was PAC AREA when this occurred) told her he would look into it. Nothing was heard since, not a word. She has followed up and nobody returns her calls. ME1 told her nobody abandoned the legacy, in fact the opposite we all were just afraid/unable to tell her.

He gave me her number and I called her immediately, told her everything and listened to her story. We are very good friends now and I speak with her and stay in contact regularly. I told her I would write everything I remembered for this book. But I also didn't want to focus on just the bad things.

I knew BM3 as "Viking Warrior," also known as Obendorf. I called him that every time I saw him in the passageways, I would deepen my voice and proclaim "The Viking Warrior has swept his domain..." when he was doing cleanups or whatever activity he was doing. I hung out with him in the gym on the WAESCHE. I didn't work out before WAESCHE, but a group of people got together and convinced me to do it. I would see Obie down there literally all the time, he lived in there it seemed. We used to razz each other for fun. I saw him on duty days and hung out and played games in the crew lounge. He was like a little brother that I saw when we weren't working. He made a shirt for our line crossing ceremony, and it had a fake button on it drawn with a sharpie, every time anyone pushed it during the ceremony he had to shout: IM A LITTLE FAT GIRL! Every time I think about that I laugh because I see his face and hear his horrible high-pitched attempt to sound like a girl. I must have pushed that button 200 times.

I remember him startling people, like a child he would hide in the closets and then jump out at people and scare them. That was funny until he did it to me. Typically, out of shock, I would punch a screaming person that jumped out at me like that. But Obie was a giant Viking. I reached back and then realized wait a sec, he is bigger than me. Another thing that stuck in my mind was that a few days before the incident happened we had an owl stay on the mast and stare into the FLIR camera mounted on the mast. Really creepy and bizarre looking and strange to see. It was there for like an hour each day just looking in at us in CIC. The FLIR is what we use to look at the sea state and small boat operations, I still think the owl was an omen of what was to come. After the incident and BM3 passed away we also had a tiny little bird with a puffed-up chest appear on the stern. This bird stayed on the boat for weeks, in storms, rough seas, it didn't matter. The little bird would sit and chirp when we went out for fresh air, there he was. The crew all started to refer to it as "The Spirit of Obie." So we named it Obie and it was there day or night sitting in its corner on the boat launch davit for 5-6 weeks, which I later realized was how long BM3 was in the hospital. I believe that bird was part of Obie staying with us and keeping an eye on us.

* * *

I RECEIVED MANY PHONE CALLS from people that weren't on the ship but involved in one way or another. I wish I could remember them all and that I had been in the frame of mind to write everything down. One that I do remember in particular, that was quite impactful, was from a young man who was actually at the D17 command center. He was a weather specialist (if I remember correctly). He said that they argued with those in charge about putting them out on the water that day. In fact, he ended up being asked to leave the room. He also stated how very wrong it all was. It never should have happened. They never should have been put out on the water...

More than one of my son's shipmates wanted me to understand that in the aftermath of the incident there were questions and concerns as to how the Command handled the investigation. I wondered about this as well. Something hadn't seemed right about any of it since the time we reached Alaska, even before that. One of the biggest questions I had was what happened to the original written statements from the crew that were ordered to be completed and handed into the Command by the next day? Those written statements were never seen again, and according to multiple crewmembers, they did not bear any resemblance to the "Summarized Statements" that were produced for the Investigation Report. Another imperative question was: why did they not take statements from the five fishermen that were involved in the rescue, or the captain of the Alaska Mist? In the investigation manuals it spells out that statements should be taken from anyone that is either directly or indirectly involved in an incident. Where are all of those statements? One crewmember told me he conversed with the Captain of the Alaska Mist, before my son was hurt, and told me that Captain was confused about why the Coast Guard was making such a big deal about the situation. Was this true?

After the accident, the Command would only tell the crew that Obie was 'doing well' and 'would be fine, yet no one could say that for sure." In reality the doctors had given a very low probability of survival for my son. It was a day-to-day fight and the command knew that. After all, SC had been in Alaska with us for over two weeks. He understood the situation. The Command should have been telling the crew the truth. Perhaps they feared a lawsuit.

I need to be clear, there are more than two friends and shipmates who came forward after the incident, both to console and to share. The two in depth accounts above standout for me for very personal reasons. Others from the crew have been such a help and a comfort, and I sincerely wish that I have helped and comforted them – this has been a tragedy for all of us.

I am so grateful to all of them for sharing with me. It became more than apparent how much they cared for Obie and the impact he had on their lives. I am so glad that he was able to share these friendships and have these people in his life. We are glad that they are in our lives as well. Thank You~

It is tough to summarize the words of so many, and maybe it's best that I don't. Many of his shipmates and friends have called me out of the blue, asking for forgiveness for the delay, and supported my conclusions on the sketchy circumstances surrounding the death of my son. Some of these shipmates have helped me with this book, some have not. I wish all of them only the best.

Many of Obie's shipmates have remained in the Coast Guard. They have families. They have children and pets. They have normal struggles and hardships. They have routines that they both enjoy and struggle with. Some have badass trucks. Some are always listening to music. Some live in the gym... Their memories of Obie and that awful day reoccur and are unrelenting. How could anyone ever be the same after experiencing what they did?

They all say: "Veterans Day is our Memorial Day."

MORE SEARCHING

Mixed Emotions

"It could have happened to any of us."
— "Empathy for Coast Guard Seaman Ethan Tucker,"
Bradley Angle

A T SOME POINT MY DAY-IN-DAY-OUT ROUTINE was only research. I wanted every detail I could find about the Coast Guard. For anyone who has done this, you'll be proud but fatigued by story after story of life saving, drug intervention adventures, and environmental mishaps. The statistics for Coast Guard success and influence are tremendous. Our service is by far a multi-functional and badass branch!

Though, if you keep searching, you'll find articles and occurrences buried beneath the photo ops and authentic valor pieces. You'll find a female Coastie who is marching in honor of those shipmates of hers who were lost to suicide. You'll find racial, gender and harassment scandals out of the Coast Guard academy. Weapon caches and government plots from Coast Guard officers on the East Coast. You'll read about hero dogs. The Coast Guard Auxiliary. About drug offenses in the junior ranks. Sex scandals on sea going units. And even murder(s) in Alaska. It's all there. The gamut of experience.

* * *

FOR THOSE WHO THINK I am being unjust. Or think I am only upset because of a one-off incident, that happened to take the life of my son, I ask you to consider other examples of the Coast Guard scandals, errors, catastrophes, and weaknesses; they have been well documented.

Bradley Angle is a blogger and author who served for five years in the Coast Guard, which more than qualifies him as a 'Coastie', and more than a decade as a captain, dockmaster, diver and operations consultant. His recent book, "Shipmates: Before the Mast: A Coastie's Chronicle of the Dishonorable," is a tell-all review of his experience with the Coast Guard. On Amazon, the book's synopsis reads:

> "Bradley Angle pulls on his enlisted experiences in the post 9/11 Coast Guard to create vivid accounts of life aboard seagoing cutters, debauched port-calls, dishonest missions, and the known and poorly managed problem of alcohol and drug abuse in the military. This is the first portrait of the enlisted Coastie, published by a former junior petty officer, without a superfluous focus on ASTs, machoism or devotion-to-duty."
>
> With a backdrop of the US Coast Guard's transition from the Department of Transportation to the more militant Department of Homeland Security, in this story of stories, the straight-out-of-boot non-rate, Pojack Ashore, rambles his way through life aboard a 378, alongside despondent shipmates and superiors. Transferring to "A" school, Pojack finds an opportunity to join one of the most elite units in the CG. At this new unit, he struggles to fight off old addictions, he's pessimistic about the new objectives of the Coast Guard, and he crafts better ways of impressing his superior officers."

It's important to think about that change of mission, which included a major change in philosophy for the Coast Guard. It had to affect everyone, for better or worse, and it created, unintentionally, opportunities for bad situations to be overlooked. In his blogs, Angle continues to talk about and bring to light many dangerous issues that need to be addressed and corrected before other Coasties meet the same fate as my son, Obie.

In a piece Angle posted to Jack's Joint, an unofficial Coast Guard Library and More, Angle cautions that there are 'official' and 'unofficial' sea stories about the Coast Guard. He believes the official stories are sanitized versions of real life in which heroism and rescue are emphasized. The unofficial version of life in the Coast Guard, according to Angle, includes "political conflict, disgruntled and depressed sailors and complete sunny day boredom".

Writing about the murder trial of Coast Guard Seaman Ethan Tucker, Angle argues that the Coast Guard ignored warning flags that signaled the impending catastrophe that was the premature death of a shipmate.

Angle goes on to expose a "toxic Coast Guard culture" that affects decision-making on many levels. In Tucker's well documented case, Angle reveals that information was continually hampered by a zero-tolerance culture in which people were unprepared and emergency response readiness was impaired. Command on many occasions accepted risks that "endangered the mental and physical health of crews; including prolonged and unnecessary deployment, unsafe and unnecessary tasks, and internal competition between commands. The charge against seaman Tucker, branded a 'renegade Coastie', should never have been made, Angle suggests. The charge "will have negative consequences throughout the Coast Guard ranks, including distrust in leadership, cynicism toward the UCMJ, suspicion of shipmates, and over-reporting and fear-of-reporting unauthorized activities".

The ordeal of Seaman Tucker is not unique, nor are the problems with the Coast Guard culture. Back in 1995, Captain Ernie Blanchard was railroaded out of service by the Coast Guard after being accused of sexual harassment during a Coast Guard Academy event. It didn't matter that Blanchard's record was exemplary or that there turned out to be no evidence against him. The Coast Guard rushed through the investigation to sweep it all under the rug. Blanchard's career was ruined. Within a year, he committed suicide, leaving behind a wife and family. Retired Navy Captain Ladson F. Mills published his book about this case in 2019: Abandoned Shipmates: The Destruction of Coast Guard Captain Ernie Blanchard.

In 2010, a report of safety markers missing from transmission lines and cables was ignored, leading to the deaths of three Coast Guard crewmen aboard an MH-60T Jayhawk helicopter, which flew straight into those wires. The helicopter's front half of its cabin shot out into the sea, killing the crewmembers. A controversial charge of negligent homicide was brought against the only crewmember to survive, yet couldn't that same charge have been levied against Command that ignored the warnings about the poorly marked lines? Later that same year, a similar Coast Guard helicopter crashed, injuring all five crewmembers.

In 2014, Vietnam Veterans of America and the Veterans Legal Services Clinic at Yale Law School published a report that proves the Coast Guard illegally discharged members for medical and adjustment disorders. The justification for this behavior, the report said, was so that the Coast Guard could save billions in veteran benefits. The report concludes that "the records analyzed in this paper demonstrate that the Coast Guard has been denying service members these essential regulatory protections and illegally discharging members for the past decade."

"When I was in the first stages of proofing my book," Angle writes, "I read a news report on a Coast Guardsman who died of unknown causes in Dutch Harbor, Alaska. I happened into a CG Patrol Boat at a San Francisco fueling dock that same day. Those Coasties and I speculated on the cause of death, reminisced over the debaucheries we'd all experienced in Unalaska/Dutch Harbor, and parted ways with agreements that it was 'just a matter of time'."

JUST A MATTER OF TIME. These words haunt me every day of my life. If only we had known better, but then, what would we have done better? Sadly, we'll never know.

* * *

J ust consider this quote from USCG Admiral James Milton Loy: "I was both astounded and grieved to read that 73% of respondents [Coasties] thought that the officers over them cared more for their own careers than for the needs of their subordinates."

This is astounding and beyond upsetting! It is also a long way from these words in the U.S. Coast Guard COMTINST M5351.3: "Leadership is the ability to influence others to obtain their obedience, respect, confidence, and loyal cooperation."

Leadership must be the heart and soul of any service; otherwise, the service fractures and falls apart. The Coast Guard, like other service branches, relies on government appropriations to finance its vast operations. With massive annual appropriations comes the necessity for round-the-clock accountability, a never-ending process that anyone who has ever served in the armed forces understands. The weight of accountability weighs heavily on the shoulders of Coast Guard Headquarters and service men and women alike, but it seems to befall the service men and women much more than CGH.

I know many people will think incidents like those that took my son's life are just tragic accidents, and it's not like they're happening every day. True. But that doesn't excuse negligence, or shrugging responsibility after something bad happens. Again, and again, as I tried to find the truth behind my son's incident, I ran up against a Command bureaucracy that misled, misstated and sometimes outright hid the truth.

I'm not saying that all the men and women in the Coast Guard Command are bad people. Overwhelmingly, they are not. Sometimes they're clipped and discarded. Sometimes they escape justice and enjoy long careers and contented retirements. Obie will enjoy neither of these.

Yes, safety and equipment changes were made after my son's death, yet they could have and should have been done before and he would still be alive. They were formally requested 4 years prior. It took a needless death before Command stepped up and did the right thing.

Why does it always seem to be that way? Isn't it antiquated to write checks in blood? Why does it have to take a death or many deaths to get someone's attention? This question haunts me and I don't know if I am any closer to an answer that makes sense. As time goes on and individuals climb up the leadership ladder there are examples that are set in place. And as more time goes on and more people see what others got away with, it just continues to get worse and it pollutes the whole institution. It seems true that institutional complacency can eat into the efficiency and morale of organizations, great and small.

It's all too rampant in Command positions in the Coast Guard. In my son's case, Command unbelievably found fault with the crew. I was outraged when the final report on Obie's incident cited the crew as being at fault and that they had made the choices that unfolded into what happened that day. I know it has caused lasting pain and professional hardships for some of the crew and Obie's other shipmates.

Everyone knew what was right. Operational guidelines were sidelined. Safety assessments were rushed, lip-served, and then ignored. Work requests were placed in filing cabinets. The crew was over-worked. The command wanted publicity. The fishing vessel wasn't taking abnormal risk. My son said: "SOMEONE'S GOING TO GET HURT ON THIS ONE."

* * *

O N JUNE 3, 2014, a good friend called me and asked if I was watching TV. I answered "no," and she said I better turn it on because an episode of Deadliest Catch was airing and Obie's incident was on it. I felt as if I was kicked in the gut.

After my son's trauma, the mission to remove fishermen from the Alaska Mist came to a standstill. The vessel stayed at anchor until the following day when a TV crew from Deadliest Catch boarded the Coast Guard helo that would go and airlift additional fishermen off the fishing boat.

After six months, Deadliest Catch, with the permission of Coast Guard public affairs office, aired the episode, along with clips of my son's Coast Guard memorial. I was never contacted by the Coast Guard or by Deadliest Catch for this.

ACCEPTANCE

We can't all be heroes because someone has to sit on the curb and clap as they go by.

—Will Rogers

THE QUOTE ABOVE WAS READ by the Vice Adm. Paul Zukunft, on January 30, 2014 during the official memorial ceremony for my son, sponsored by the Coast Guard aboard the Waesche. It is unfortunate Zukunft attributed the quote to Mark Twain. But it's only a quote. *Just words.*

Other words I hear often, especially on Coast Guard online forums, is *"YOU HAVE TO GO OUT, BUT YOU DON'T HAVE TO COME BACK."* That phrase makes me cry. Well, it makes me sick mostly, but I always cry. Then there is the *"IT'S WHAT HE SIGNED UP FOR."* Or, *"SERVICE ABOVE SELF."*

They are all words. Does anyone really think about them? Do people care to think about what they say, and the implications of these phrases?

My son was sensitive – THE GENTLE GIANT. During his memorial service aboard the Coast Guard Cutter Waesche, he was described as an avid hunter and fisherman, but that was so far from the truth. Obie hated the thought of harming any animal. He loved animals, they were drawn to him all his life, children in much the same way. He understood them, never talking down to them or brushing them off. Children and animals alike know when a person is authentic or phony, when a person genuinely cares about them. They knew Obie cared about them.

One of his affectionate nicknames aboard the Waesche was THE HULK. The crew said that the gym was his second home. In fact, one of his shipmates was allowed to paint his portrait on the gym door of the Waesche after he passed away, she was painting it while we were there for the memorial. It's still there to this day. He stood six feet and weighed a buff 225. If he wasn't gaming, then Obie would be in the gym pumping iron, listening to his music.

My son was a giver, always. While in his early years in the Coast Guard, he volunteered to help with clean-up after an oil spill. His job was to pick up globs of oil from the sandy beach, but he wanted to help animals and people more directly. He was still glad that he was there and helping in some way, but just a little frustrated he couldn't do it in a more direct manner.

I have had so many impactful experiences since I lost Trav. I've met many, very kind, caring, compassionate people. My family and friends have wanted and tried to do everything possible to help with the pain, and I thank them all. I know this is something that people struggle with. It's not the normal situation or everyday process. Our children aren't supposed to go before us. People in our society are uncomfortable with death to begin with and then you put losing-a-child equation into it and it's even more uncomfortable for them. I have had people, that I have known for years, look the other way and avoid me in stores so that they didn't have to talk to me.

I finally went to see a counselor for some help six months after we had lost Trav. Sometime into the session, she said to me "Laurie, *IT'S BEEN SIX MONTHS,*" as if I was supposed to be over it. Maybe people don't realize that this is something that never goes away, this isn't something that you get over. You're able to move forward at some point, but you just don't get over the loss of a child. I found a saying from a parent that had lost a child and it is one that I have to remind myself of often: "It doesn't get better, it just gets different." I wake up every morning knowing that I will spend another day without my son. I go to bed every night knowing that I have to get up and face the next day without my son. There are no words to describe how much I miss him.

It took me awhile to come out of my cave after I lost Trav and be amongst the real world. I thought that getting back to work might help. Chad and I live in a very small community and the majority of the work here is seasonal, with world renowned fishing and many tourists. So, I set out one afternoon in search of a job. The man that owned the establishment I happened into was a retired Army Lieutenant, if I remember correctly, ex-military anyway. He and his wife had lost a child also, not military related, however still very tragic. His wife introduced us and she told him that I had lost my son while serving in the Coast Guard. He laughed and said "*WELL I GUESS HE SERVED HIS COUNTRY,*" with a definite question mark hanging in the air. I was so stunned! Why do people think this way? Do they think, because he was in the Coast Guard, the meaning of his service and loss of his life meant less? How can this be?

Some of the worst, heartbreaking and insulting interactions I've experienced have been from people in the military community. Not all; I have met some very wonderful people as well – mothers and fathers that have lost their children and my heart breaks with theirs!

On two separate occasions, retired Marines have come to my home to deliver things. They saw Trav's tribute room and his photo hanging on the wall. On both instances they laughed. One said *"HUH...THE COAST GUARD."*

I have approached retired, elderly men in the grocery store, wearing their particular military branch veterans' hats, and thanked them for their service, saying also that my son was in the Coast Guard, not sharing anything else. Most have just walked away without any response at all. Why is this? Why does it have to be this way? My son's death doesn't mean any less just because he wasn't carrying a gun into battle! Truth be known he did carry a gun, they all carry a gun, and they are on their own battlefield day in and day out, you just don't hear about it.

So, I trouble over these words and phrases. These lip-service recognitions and, worse, down-right rude assumptions. What does anyone know who refuses to ponder? Empty words, are what bring out the sadness.

But there are words that are representative of something tangible! The mighty words that I see everywhere are HONOR, RESPECT, DEVOTION TO DUTY. These are not just words for me. These are the conceptual ideals of my son. These words are salutes to the people who do care, who fight for principle above rank, respect above promotion, patience in the storm.

Poetry in prose and in lyrics are a love I share with my son. Trav and I still share the magic of poems, verse and lyrics.

I was told of a phrase that Coasties referred to when speaking of the National Security Cutters (WMSLs). Those that served on the Waesche defined WMSL as: *WHERE I LOST MY SOUL.* How very sad is that?

* * *

CHAD AND I HELD a Remembrance here at our home on the 5-year anniversary of the incident. Obie's friend and shipmate JT asked if we could put something together on the 5-year anniversary, so that more people could possibly get some peace and experience some healing. He felt he was able to do this when he came to visit us and he wanted that for the others. Of course, we were on board, we also wanted to do something to honor Trav. These people needed a chance to grieve and we had not held any sort of memorial or remembrance for Obie. It was held on November 11, 2018. We had 17 Coasties at our home and it was wonderful! Our small community did everything in their power to accommodate and make it possible for us to host the remembrance for Obie. We visited the memorial tree that was planted for him along the river in Idaho Falls. One of Obie's friends that is now a fireman arranged to have their boom truck there when everyone arrived with a huge American Flag flying from it – there was a number of police and firemen there as well. I was very grateful for their efforts and it meant a lot to the Coasties. They built massive bonfires in the firepit next door where Obie's platform, bench and flagpole are. Everyone hung out, reconnected, cried and talked. It was a 4-day event and on Saturday evening each one, one by one, sat down with me and told me of his or her experience. We cried, we hugged. I thanked them all for being his friends and family and of course for coming to honor and remember him. I hope they experienced some sort of healing from that day, some semblance of peace. At least that was the outcome that we had hoped for, for them all.

The one thing that was said across the board was that this never should have happened! They never should have been put out on the water that day. Ego took over and nothing else mattered. Numbers and promotions were on the line and took precedence over safety and the wellbeing of the crew. It was chaotic and the command lost control of the whole situation. They all shared the same story, not to mention all of the phone calls that I had received telling me the same thing. But they all feared for their careers if they spoke out or put anything in writing, and I understand. Even those that were out of the CG were afraid of what might happen to them.

* * *

T HE COAST GUARD REMEMBERS OBIE. Aboard the Waesche, despite their continuing heavy deployment schedule, they have tried to keep his memory alive. The "Waesche Spirit of Obie" award is given out quarterly, to junior ranking shipmates who've gone above and beyond. The door of the gym is painted as a tribute to my son. A plaque with Obie's photo is on the mess deck. And as of late 2020 there is a granite bench at the base in Alameda, looking out over the water, thanks to the very hard work of Obie's friends and shipmates.

The Coast Guard paid for us to attend multiple memorials, including the National Law Enforcement Memorial, where my son's name was etched onto the wall, along with all of the other hero's that have lost their lives. They flew us to Grand Haven for the Coast Guard's annual festival. Not to mention our accommodation's while we were standing vigil beside Trav for 38 days. We know this isn't a common occurrence. For all of these things we are very grateful.

* * *

I HAVE BEEN ASKED to explain my motives behind the book. Why the book? Why now? Why bring all of this up now? Why question the decisions of the command and those in charge after the fact? My response has always been and remains: the most valuable return for this is Lessons Learned: How to treat the subordinates below you, how to respect their positions, respect them as people and not let your ego take over. Those coming up in command, check your ego at the door. Don't expect respect, earn respect. I can't let Obie's death be taken in vain.

People have turned on me and never spoken to me again because they feel that we are doing the wrong thing by telling the truth and trying to bring just a little shred of justice for Obie and what he went through; telling the truth for the decency and peace of mind of the crew. When did it become so wrong to tell the truth? NEVER!

The service should be honest and transparent. Unfortunately, it was not consistently honest and transparent after my son's fatal incident, nor has it been in others. My greatest grief and frustration was losing my son, of course, but I've also been tormented by the way the formal investigation was conducted and the way the CG treated my son's shipmates. The investigation effectively silenced many crewmembers, misled and concealed certain facts that came to light much later. Worst of all, the investigation gave the Command a pass and actually blamed the crew instead. The results of the investigation have continued to hurt those brave crewmembers and others aboard the Waesche to this day. Depression, anxiety, guilt and PTSD are just some of the issues that those affected have had to deal with in their lives since Obie's passing. The Coast Guard, I believe, should have assigned blame for the incident where blame was due—the Command. Blame should never be assigned to the crew, which operated heroically in challenging conditions and with faulty equipment under the orders of the command.

Some people may say that I am making too much of this, that I should let it go and GET ON WITH MY LIFE. This sort of thing happens all the time in the military "IT'S WHAT THEY SIGNED UP FOR," I have been told. Yes, sadly it happens all too often in the military. To all of those that have lost a loved one, my heart aches with you. My grief has been deep, so deep that there have been times I wondered if I would ever see the light of day again. It has not been easy, going on and repairing my life. It's not easy to this day. Yet, I believe in my son's legacy, his heroism and in the heroic mission of the Coast Guard in which he served. I also believe in transparency and truth. I want the truth. Isn't that what everyone deserves?

I hope that going forward the Coast Guard would be fiercely and bravely honest in every situation, after every incident, in every investigation, regardless of what it pertains to or the circumstances, so that mothers, fathers, brothers, sisters, grandparents, cousins, nephews, nieces and friends will never know the suffering that I, my family and Obie's friends and shipmates have endured.

So, this is our story: Obie's story, my story, our family's story. It also belongs to my son's shipmates and friends. His command too, and all that have served their country and all that have suffered loss, sometimes supreme loss. This book is for anyone who believes in truth and has the integrity to tell it.

God bless all of you!

Eternally Grateful,

Laurie Powell, December 18, 2020

PART 4

For the Record

FOR THE RECORD

A T NO POINT WAS IT EASY TO CREATE THIS BOOK. The idea was generated years ago, maybe it was the release of the official investigation (MII) that sparked my decision – it certainly sparked my decision to do my own investigating. Before that, "denial" was the typical diagnosis I was given by the embarrassed eyes of friends and loved ones, or directly by my therapist. But even the USCG MII agreed that my son did not have to go out, and he could have come back, if only the command had listened to the crew and decommissioned the faulty equipment. So where is the justice? It was the thought that ruled my mind – it had complete control over me. Slowly, with the help of Obie's shipmates and close friends and family, we groomed our emotional landscape into something useable, and with this book – tangible. The question is not "where is the justice," we've answered that. The question now is, who will accept it? Who will learn the lessons? I hope this book helps.

For most of you, I believe my words alone are not sufficient, and I cannot blame you. So, I've shared some of the documents and stories that I received along the way. Below are the more-or-less unedited, though reformatted, materials that had the most significant impact in my search. I will leave names out, to protect everyone.

Following:

- USCG's Major Incident Investigation Board Report
- FOIA Request
- Emails from the Day of Incident
- Thoughts from My Son's Shipmates and Friends

USCG – MAJOR INCIDENT INVESTIGATION[7]

SUBJECT: (MII) BOARD REPORT REGARDING THE CIRCUMSTANCES OF THE CASUALTY TO CGC WAESCHE'S SRP 24104 & INJURIES TO A SMALLBOAT CREWMEMBER ON 11 NOVEMBER 13

MISSION: On 10 November 2013, Coast Guard District 17 informed the Coast Guard Cutter Waesche (WAESCHE) that a fishing vessel (F/V) had lost propulsion and a commercial towing vessel was dispatched to assist. At that time, the information from District 17 was advisory in nature, and WAESCHE was told to continue with its plan to disembark its helicopter the following day and proceed to Dutch Harbor for a planned port call.

Early on 11 November 2013, (Veterans Day) District 17 contacted WAESCHE to inform the ship that the commercial towing vessel had experienced a casualty and would be unable to assist the disabled F/V. The new report now had the F/V approximately 8.5 NM from land and drifting towards shore at a speed of 1.5 knots. District 17 then directed WAESCHE to make best, safe speed to the F/V which was approximately 160 miles away from the cutter's position and conduct the SAR response. At the reported drift rate, WAESCHE would not reach the F/V before it would run aground. However, the drift rate of the vessel was continually updated that morning, and the F/V was eventually able to anchor successfully while drifting. While the F/V was anchored, it was not clear if or for how long the anchor would continue to hold if weather worsened over time, so WAESCHE continued to prepare for the worst-case scenario. The sea conditions at the time were rough, and based on the weather predictions the seas were expected to abate throughout the day and while transiting east. After sunrise on 11 November 2013, improving weather allowed WAESCHE to increase speed and advance the arrival time from 4:00 p.m. to about 2:30 p.m. WAESCHE's Commanding Officer wanted to arrive as early as possible in order to maximize daylight throughout the operation; sunset was forecast for 6:10 p.m. that day. Meanwhile, WAESCHE began preparations for the SAR operation: a brief was held with First Lieutenant, Chief Boatswain's Mate, department heads, Executive Officer, and Commanding Officer to develop detailed questions for the F/V master prior to conducting a passenger transfer or tow. The answers would help WAESCHE determine the best method to conduct the SAR response.

After arrival on scene, WAESCHE planned to conduct a situational assessment. If conditions allowed, the plan was to transfer all non-essential crew members from the disabled F/V via WAESCHE's mishap SRP, which would require three trips. District 17 requested the removal of non-essential personnel from the fishing vessel to mitigate future risk in the event the F/V broke free from its anchored position and ran aground or began taking on water once it was being towed. On the first trip, the mishap SRP would disembark a WAESCHE crew member aboard the F/V with several sets of personal protective equipment, including Anti-exposure Coveralls for the F/V crew members. A WAESCHE crew member would remain on board in order to assist the F/V

---

[7] The full document can be found at https://media.defense.gov/2017/Oct/05/2001823261/-1/-1/0/FINALACTIONMIIBOARDREPORTSIGNED.PDF or by a quick google search (1/8/21)

crew with the towing bridle. The mishap SRP would then embark the F/V non-essential personnel and deliver them back to WAESCHE. The ship planned to conduct three personnel transfers that afternoon using the mishap SRP: five civilian personnel on the first trip, five on the second, and four on the final trip. WAESCHE also planned to use the small boat to transfer the tow line messenger to the F/V. However, if necessary, WAESCHE was also prepared to use a line throwing gun to facilitate the transfer of the messenger to the F/V. Once a tow was successfully initiated, WAESCHE planned to take the F/V in tow back to Dutch Harbor.

The F/V was a 167 foot vessel and displaced 916 gross tons. WAESCHE has a towing capacity of 4,000 long tons; the F/V was well within WAESCHE's capability to tow. Based on a self-reported condition, the F/V was considered seaworthy despite its loss of propulsion. After attempting to anchor while drifting for several hours, the F/V reported being anchored with six shots (540 feet) of anchor chain in approximately 130 feet of water with a rocky bottom. While the fishing vessel was anchored, the scope of chain normally considered for reliable anchoring is five-to-seven times the depth of water. In this case, the F/V used four times the depth of water for their anchor chain scope. While the anchor held the F/V in position at the time, it was unknown how long the anchor would hold.

PLANNING & PREPARATION: WAESCHE conducted a weather brief, tow brief, and boat brief in succession starting at 1:00 p.m. on the mess deck of the cutter. The weather brief was provided by embarked naval weather specialist, who predicted the following conditions: mostly cloudy with patchy mist and light rain; visibility ranging from unrestricted to 3 to 5 NM; air temperatures 35 to 45 degrees Fahrenheit; and winds 18 to 23 kts, decreasing to 8 to 13 kts. The tow brief was conducted by the First Lieutenant, and the small boat Coxswain conducted the small boat brief. Earlier in the day, Operations Officer and Commanding Officer selected WAESCHE's most experienced and skilled Coxswain for the evolution. The briefs were widely attended by participants in the planned operations that day aboard WAESCHE, including Commanding Officer, Executive Officer, Operations Officer, Officer-of-the-Deck, and Conning Officer in addition to appropriate members involved in the planned evolutions.

The GAR risk assessment score for the tow brief was 32 out of 70 based on seven district criteria, with highs in environment (six on a scale of ten) and evolution complexity (eight of ten). A score of 32 out of 70 is considered a "low" Amber risk assessment. The following concerns were voiced and discussed during the risk assessment: towing was not a commonly conducted evolution on WAESCHE; the F/V would not have concurrent set and drift with WAESCHE because it was at anchor; environmental conditions were not ideal. The possibility of using a helicopter to perform the personnel transfer was also raised, and it was noted that District 17 had two helicopters located in Cold Bay. However, based on the risk assessment, the Commanding Officer supported the plan to remove the non-essential personnel by boat.

The boat brief GAR score was 22 out of 60 based on six distinct criteria, with high scores in environment (seven of ten) and event complexity (five of ten). A score of 22 is considered a "high" Green risk assessment. The launch and recovery of the mishap SRP from WAESCHE were not considered significant risks by crewmembers attending the brief. WAESCHE had operated in the District 17 AOR for nearly three months by the time of this operation. They had executed 130 safe boat launch and recovery evolutions from the stern notch of the ship, including four operations within the previous five weeks which involved a sea state exceeding the parameters of the mishap

SRP, according to WAESCHE's logs. For WAESCHE's crew, utilizing the stern notch for small boat operations in these circumstances was not unusual.

The primary risk addressed during the GAR discussion was the personnel transfer of civilians off of the F/V and onto the mishap SRP. WAESCHE planned to transfer non-essential personnel from the F/V in three groups (two groups of five, one group of four). There were two civilians identified with slight injuries, one with a hurt leg and one with a hurt finger. However, both were ambulatory and would be transferred as part of the first group.

As with most of the other small boat operations during WAESCHE's District 17 patrol, the plan was to launch the small boat from the stern notch of the cutter. WAESCHE's command and crew generally accept the use of the stern notch as the safer mode of launch and recovery compared with the alternative, starboard side, single point davit. The ship's single-point davit had an unreliable constant-tension function (making heavy weather operation comparatively riskier), requires more people to operate, and requires use of Jacob's ladder to transfer excess passengers. The use of Jacob's ladder is also considered more difficult and less safe on a WMSL class ship due to the tumblehome hull profile. During the small boat brief, Commanding Officer stated that if the evolution was deemed to be unsafe, they would postpone the passenger transfer until the morning, or the tow could also be accomplished with a line throwing gun if the cutter was unable to launch the small boat.

After the briefings were completed, WAESCHE arrived on-scene with the F/V. At the time, the Operations Officer briefed the conditions and cutter status to D17 and received concurrence to proceed.

Boat deck positions were not assigned prior to setting the boat detail; qualified members knew what roles they generally took and all were filled at the time of the evolution via a volunteer process overseen by Chief Boatswain's Mate. Members of the boat detail were taken from the towing crew since it takes only two members to launch the small boat, in addition to the safety officers. Both Boatswain's Mate and First Lieutenant served as safety officers for the towing and small boat launch and recovery operations. A First-Class Boatswain's Mate served as Deck-In-Charge, providing all boat deck launch and recovery directions.

The Conning Officer and other bridge positions were predetermined in advance of the operations. Communications between the bridge and the fantail occurred via the ship's handheld "HYDRA" VHF Radios and involve talking with the Deck Safety Officer, usually First Lieutenant. The bridge Officer-of-the-Deck talks with the Deck-In-Charge, and the Deck-In-Charge reports when the small boat deck is manned and ready. The deck indicates readiness to open the stern doors before the crew is in the boat, ready to launch, permission to launch, and away. The communications are not scripted, but typically there is conversation between the bridge and the boat deck about whether ship's course is good for launching the small boat. Communications with small boat are maintained by personnel in the ship's combat information center (CIC), and the bridge monitors those communications as well. The bridge communicates with the small boat through CIC.

The Cutter Operations Bill states in part that the Commanding Officer may need to make a launch/no launch comprehensive assessment based on, "urgency of mission, wave shape and period, seas, wind, visibility, temperature, experience and proficiency of boat crew and launch/recovery detail, fatigue, duration of mission/transit distance, improving vs. deteriorating conditions, etc. that should be considered when operating beyond the limits defined in policy.

Based on WAESCHE's logs, the mishap SRP was operating beyond its sea/swell height parameters; however, the additional indicators were part of the Commanding Officer's comprehensive assessment to launch the mishap SRP in the final moments before directing the boat launch.

ACCIDENT SUMMARY: After the boat brief, the mishap Coxswain began his preparations and donned his dry suit. He did not feel rushed and took his time getting ready for the mission. However, Deck-In-Charge received multiple communications from the bridge requesting the readiness status of the mishap SRP crew. The Deck-In-Charge perceived that the bridge was anxious to get the operation started in order to maximize daylight. The ship pipped the Coxswain to report to the fantail, and he arrived at the stern notch where his crew was standing by ready in the small boat. All members of the mishap SRP were prepared and wearing appropriate PPE, including Special Operations Headset Adaptable Helmets. The fantail relayed recommendations for a boat launch course to the bridge, and the Coxswain got the mishap SRP underway using normal launching procedures.

After the mishap SRP launched, WAESCHE altered its course in order to station-keep and observe the small boat and F/V operations. The station-keeping course allowed swells to surge into the stern notch, and the fantail requested to close the ship's stern doors. The Officer-of-the-Deck and Deck-In-Charge discussed expediting the evolutions in order to preserve as much daylight as possible, and the decision was made by the Commanding Officer to keep the stern doors open during the operation. The stern doors on the WAESCHE normally take two to three minutes to close or open. The bridge personnel also observed the swells and the Officer-of-the-Deck ordered boat deck personnel inside the skin of the ship while the mishap SRP was away.

The Coxswain brought the mishap SRP alongside the disabled F/V. He observed significant sea swells but also noticed the swells had a long-period between them, which made them easier than short-period swells to negotiate. The Coxswain developed a plan for the personnel transfer from the port side of the F/V and received permission from WAESCHE to proceed with the plan. After embarking a crew member onto the F/V, the Coxswain recalled it took about 25 minutes to start the transfer of passengers from the F/V to the mishap SRP. While waiting, the Coxswain observed an increase in wind speed, and he called back to the cutter stating that he wanted to reassess weather conditions upon return to WAESCHE. Once the five civilian passengers were embarked in the mishap SRP, the Coxswain navigated back to WAESCHE.

While the mishap SRP was alongside of the F/V, the Conning Officer began maneuvering the ship to the south of the F/V's position in order to provide the mishap SRP crew with a shorter distance, down swell ride upon return. The Conning Officer reported that he did not see any appreciable difference in the seas or weather throughout the operation, and the primary and secondary swells were the predominant factors in the chosen recovery course. The Conning Officer maneuvered WAESCHE back to the same heading used during the launch of the mishap SRP, and the ship was making five to six knots of speed, which was deemed to be the optimal course and speed for boat launch and recovery operations by the WAESCHE's leadership. Once the Conning Officer maneuvered to the recovery course, the First Lieutenant confirmed that the course was acceptable with the Deck-In-Charge and Deck Safety. The First Lieutenant generally gives a recommended course correction if the ship's course does not appear to be appropriate for a given small boat operation.

During the transit back to WAESCHE, the mishap Coxswain noted additional confused seas while crossing the wake on the starboard side of the cutter. The Coxswain initially lined up the mishap SRP about 50 to 100 yards aft of WAESCHE. While positioned behind the cutter, he observed a large swell surge into the stern of the ship. About 30 seconds later he received permission to enter the notch and began his approach. recovery due to frequent problems with slippage of the cutter's capture line system. During the recovery phase, the mishap Victim was positioned on the bow of the mishap SRP, kneeling down just forward of the center console. The mishap Victim was positioned there in order to assist with securing the capture line over the bow capture horn on the mishap SRP. WAESCHE informally developed the practice of placing a crewman up front on small boats during notch recovery due to frequent problems with slippage of the cutter's capture line system. During the recovery phase, no one on the fantail requested or proposed a course change to the bridge that would produce better conditions. It is important to note that the fantail is not required by Coast Guard policy to make course change proposals; however, it is common practice for the fantail to make recommendations to the bridge if they think a course or speed change by the ship would improve boat launch or recovery conditions. By all accounts WAESCHE's course and speed were considered optimal in the prevailing conditions.

As the Coxswain maneuvered the mishap SRP into the notch, the boat surged as it was pushed forward by a swell. The Coxswain felt the stern rise up and he "dropped the bucket" or placed the mishap SRP jet propulsion in reverse. However, the swell caused the stern to rise and the bow to drop down. As a result, the capture net and line slid over the bow horn. The net and line then struck the mishap Victim frontally but he was able to recover. Within a matter of seconds another larger swell surged into the notch pushing the mishap SRP forward again but this time with much greater force. As the mishap SRP surged forward, the net and capture line slammed into the upper body, face and head of the mishap Victim, pinning him against the center console. This time the mishap Victim's body went limp and he collapsed to the deck. The Coxswain immediately switched focus, left the controls, and began moving the injured crew member to safety away from the bow.

Immediately after the mishap, the Conning Officer observed that a tertiary swell appeared to be coming out of the northeast. The fantail radioed to the bridge that the ship needed to change course and come up in speed. The Conning Officer immediately ordered the course change and came about approximately 30 or more degrees to starboard and increased speed to further limit the seas coming into the notch.

The stern door operator was unable to immediately close the doors because the mishap SRP had not fully entered the notch. Several more swells surged into the notch in quick succession. When the carriage winch was three quarters of the way up, the controls stalled, and the carriage needed to be stopped and started again. The Fantail Carriage Operator had performed this function eight to ten times previously, and he noted that this was the first time that he had needed to reset the carriage assembly. Once the carriage pulled the mishap SRP forward of the notch threshold, the stern doors were energized and began closing.

RESPONSE ACTIONS: Within moments after the mishap, members of the WAESCHE battle dress station (BDS) medical detail responded to provide the mishap Victim with medical support. The BDS team included, among others, three trained emergency medical technicians (EMT). One of the BDS members, a First-Class Maritime Enforcement Specialist (ME1), was present on the fantail during portions of the operations that day and was nearby when he heard yelling from the fantail. The ME1 immediately donned a personal flotation device (PFD) realizing he would need to get to the boat deck to assist. At that point, the stern doors were still open and he stood close by until the seas were favorable enough for him to move down. When the boat was steady enough, the ME1 moved down to the small boat to assess the mishap Victim. He observed significant injuries and began to provide medical support. Another EMT trained BDS member also arrived and began to assist the ME1 with medical care. A stretcher was provided to the BDS members and the mishap Victim was transferred from the boat deck to the BDS station located on WAESCHE's mess deck. The BDS team observed no other significant injuries to the individuals on board the mishap SRP.

The cutter contacted District 17 to request a MEDEVAC helicopter. District 17 had two helicopters based at Cold Bay and launched an MH-65 helicopter to airlift WAESCHE's injured crewmember. Once the helicopter was close, BDS started the transport of the mishap Victim to the flight deck. Once the BDS reached the hangar, they performed another set of vitals. The helicopter arrived at the cutter at approximately 4:25 p.m., approximately 65 minutes after the mishap.

Once on scene, the MH-65 helicopter conducted a basket hoist of the injured crewmember from the flight deck. The helicopter then returned to Cold Bay where the patient was transferred to a MEDEVAC flight and flown to Anchorage. Despite the tragic outcome, the mishap Victim's treating doctors noted that the excellent initial care the Victim received from the BDS team played a significant role in keeping the patient stable and offered him the very best possible chance of surviving his serious head trauma.

The following morning, an MH-60 Coast Guard helicopter removed the remaining non-essential personnel from the F/V, then picked up the five F/V crewmembers from the WAESCHE, and flew them all to Cold Bay. The WASCHE then took the F/V in tow and had an uneventful transit back to Dutch Harbor.

The mishap victim remained in intensive care for several weeks after the incident. Although he was wearing a helmet at the time of the incident, the trauma to his head was of such severity that he succumbed to his injuries on 18 December 2013.

HUMAN FACTOR ANALYSIS: There are two human factors that made indirect contributions to the mishap. The first is channelized attention. WAESCHE's command and crew participated in the GAR risk assessment, and the testimony of the participants revealed that when discussing the environmental complexity and risk of the mission, there was a focus on discussing the challenges of the boat transfer of F/V personnel from the F/V to the mishap SRP. While there was certainly risk associated with at-sea transfers of personnel, testimony revealed the absence of substantive discussion regarding the risk associated with the boat returning to WAESCHE and entering the notch. It is my opinion that since WAESCHE had conducted 130 small boat launch and recovery operations in the previous 90 days of this patrol, they were familiar with the evolution, which facilitated this channelized attention on the F/V personnel transfers during their GAR risk discussion.

The second human factor resulted from an apparent overvaluing of platform capabilities. There are two platform limitations for conducting boat operations from the notch that are relevant in this case. First is the ships' pitch limitation of five degrees and roll limitation of six degrees. Neither testimony nor ship's log explicitly reveal whether the pitch and roll limitations were exceeded since that data is not recorded; the general sense of the testimony suggests that neither the bridge nor the fantail personnel believed the ship was operating outside of pitch or roll parameters. Given the prevailing weather at the time, it is reasonable to conclude they were operating near those limits.

The second is the SRP boat limitation of eight-foot seas. Testimony did not reveal that the sea state at the time of launch was discussed between bridge or fantail personnel, however The Commanding Officer made it clear that during the small boat brief that if he deemed the evolution to be unsafe, he would postpone the personnel transfer until the morning. The Commanding Officer's judgement in this case would take not only the sea state into consideration, but also a variety of other environmental factors to include the swell period and the ability to position WAESCHE relative to the environmental conditions in order to mitigate the operation. Despite this application of the Commanding Officer's understanding of WAESCHE's performance and sea sense, there appear to be less-well-understood performance dynamics in National Security Cutter hull design with respect to the periods at, near or beyond the limits of safe operation. In long period swells, which are common in this operating area, the size of the seas and swells can many times be managed with the optimal course and speed of the ship and well-timed execution of boat launch and recovery. Similar to the channelized attention dynamic, the overhauling of platform capabilities is facilitated by months of operating in the same geographic area and indirectly played a contributing role in this mishap.

* * *

THAT IS IT. These are portions of the report the Coast Guard has published, to allow the Command to move forward, and to bury my son.

My sources have told me that the Commanding Officer did not say in the boat briefing that, "if he deemed the evolution to be unsafe, he would postpone the personnel transfer until morning." What I was told he did say is that, "if they wouldn't do it [the crew chosen] then he would find someone that would."

I will leave it up to you, the reader, to decide what might have actually taken place. What would the crew have to gain by saying that they didn't feel comfortable with the operation and that they were basically forced into it, despite the objections and concerns of the most experienced Coxswain on board? I can certainly see what the Commanding Officer would have to gain by telling the investigator what he did; after all, those are regulations. He would not want to reveal as having gone against regulations. Not one member of the command would want that. Remember, they all played a part in this tragedy.

It's my belief that this is why Command had to shift the focus and blame back on the crew because Command ultimately did go against a number of regulations on that day, which resulted in the death of my son.

It cannot be stated strongly enough that all conducted briefs and weather conditions preceding the mission should have resulted in a Command decision to stand down. The GAR risk assessment rated high in environment and evolution complexity. There existed the option of using helicopters to remove the non-essential personnel from the fishing vessel, but the Commanding Officer told Incident Management that he wanted to remove the personnel with the small craft, even though the sea conditions were not safe to do so.

The Cutter Boat Operations Bill states that in part the Commanding Officer may need to make a launch/no launch comprehensive assessment based on, "urgency of mission, wave shape and period, seas, wind, visibility, temperature, experience and proficiency of boat crew and launch/recovery detail, fatigue, duration of mission/transit distance, improving vs. deteriorating conditions, etc." All of these should be considered when operating boats beyond the limits defined by policy regulations. Based on the logs of the Waesche, the SRP was operating beyond its sea/swell height parameters; however, these same indicators were part of the Commanding Officer's comprehensive assessment to launch the SRP right before directing the boat launch. The CO also considered the malfunctioning equipment.

The investigative report also states: according to Chapter 21 of TP-7525, the stern ramp system is designed to allow for launch and retrieval of the cutter small boats in up to mid sea state 5 on the Beaufort Scale by use of a center-line stern ramp. The ramp includes a capture mechanism that "automates the capture process and removes manual steps that would impose safety hazards to personnel." The capture system was not mission capable at the time of the "mishap". The capture line on the Waesche did not function as designed.

Waesche's sister ships, Bertholf and Stratton, also had issues with the capture line failure, however they did not implement the practice of placing a crewmember in the bow of their small boats during the notching process in order to overcome the functional deficiencies in their capture line system. Both of the sister ships' systems malfunctioned, but worked between 80 and 90% of the time. Waesche's worked only 40% of the time.

On November 11th the crew of the rescue craft said the environmental conditions were not the worst the cutter had encountered during the patrol, but it was rough. The waves were confused and the period varied. Swell waves were recorded at twelve feet. The Coxswain for the SAR was chosen due to his experience and the weather conditions. He was considered the most capable person for the operation on the ship, as well as the other crew members on the mission. The Hulk was chosen because he was the best man for the job – to compensate for the failures of the command and CGH.

The investigative report concluded that there was "channelized attention" being paid to the transfer of personnel from the fishing vessel and not to the overall operation, as in the sea conditions and the small boat being able to return and enter the stern notch safely. Given the prevailing weather conditions at the time, Command sent the rescue craft out to operate outside of the parameters of the ship for conducting a small boat operation. The small boat's limitations were also overlooked. The craft was not rated to function in seas exceeding eight feet. When Conn reported to the Bridge, he observed swells of twelve feet or greater coming out of the Northwest, but the seas were confused, with secondary swells coming from the South. Winds were 20-25 knots with gusts to 30 knots. Conn stated that a primary concern with the launch/recovery of the small boat was the pitch parameter of the ship. Even a seasoned Conning Officer would have struggled with the conditions that day. Sources told me that the Conning Officer chosen for this SAR had recently qualified. Why did the Command insist on the most experienced Coxswain for the operation, but was okay with a Conning Officer that had just qualified?

There were numerous requests from the Boat Deck Supervisor and Safety Supervisor to close the stern doors because of the deteriorating sea. All were denied.

Summarized testimony from the Engineer Officer said that while talking with ME1 on the fantail, the EO also observed that waves were surging into the notch. He had never seen waves enter the stern that high before; every 10th to 20th wave would flood up to the boat deck. EO spoke to BMC telling him that they would need to close the door. BMC said he had asked twice, for the stern doors to be closed, but the bridge insisted they keep the stern doors open in order to expedite the recovery of the small boat/mission.

I found a notice at the back of the investigative report indicating that the stern notch doors had also been malfunctioning.

I happened to notice that the Investigation Guidelines were amended for this particular Investigation. Why? The Vice Admiral/Commander of Pacific Area was the Convening Authority of the investigation. The Vice Admiral/Commander of Pacific Area, also had the authority to amend the Guidelines for the Investigation. All of the people involved in the outcome of the Internal Investigation and following MII report, were also people who made decisions effecting the outcome of the incident being investigated. How is this not an obvious and unethical conflict of interest? Of course no one was held accountable.

Many of the crew were not interviewed during the investigative process; others found that their testimonies were somehow not included in the report. How could this happen? The five fishermen that were brought over from the F/V and were on the craft would have been first-hand eyewitnesses. Why were they not included in the investigation? What about the Captain of the F/V? What about a representative from Deadliest Catch, or at least the communications between that organization and the Coast Guard! There are so many questions that were raised from all of this, so many unanswered questions. A statement from a retired CG Boatswain's Mate could not have said it better: *"SOMEONE REALLY LET THIS YOUNG MAN DOWN."*

Once the Summarized Testimonies were completed by the Investigator, they were not given back to the witnesses to sign off on. Most were stunned when they saw what their testimony said in the investigation results.

Command ordered written statements be submitted to them within the first 24 hours of the incident. This timeframe actually preceded the arrival a week after the incident of the Investigator on board. No one will acknowledge what became of those original statements. I do know they were not the same as the statements that became part of the official record in the investigative report. Did it factor into play that one of the "officers" on the WAESCHE who was directly involved in the operation was also an attorney?

In an April 24th, 2014 article for KUCB—Alaska, author Lauren Rosenthal reported that, according to Chief Warrant Officer Allyson Conroy, "cutters formally requested improvements to the boat capture system about four years ago"—long before my son and his rescue crewmates were thrust into harm's way. "The safety implications were not evident at that particular time," Conroy said. This assertion begs the question—if 'the safety implications were not evident', why was the request for improvements to the capture system made in the first place? "Of course," Conroy continued, "retrospectively, the changes were incorrectly prioritized among numerous high-priority configuration change projects." This waffling is accurate, but it is also Command doublespeak for 'We really fucked up here'.

If there is a neutral way of saying that, please, someone tell me. A healthy, happy, productive young man, my son, lost his life because of an event that never should have happened. Obie died because the Command he trusted and obeyed let him down. The result was devastating for him, his family, friends and shipmates. For all but Obie, who of course paid the ultimate price—his life—the emotional devastation continues. But in contrast to those lives, the lives and careers of Command personnel, literally unscathed by the tragedy, have gone on with promotions and decorations.

I am willing to admit here, even as a grieving mother, that there was no premeditation, no intention to do harm on the day the Waesche launched its rescue vehicle. Incompetence at certain levels did play important roles in what happened that day, but it was not the crew that should have been singled out for negligence and blame. It is a fact that Command is always responsible for its crew and institutions. If there are weak or compromised links in the chain of leadership, the command is responsible. A command's failures will always invite and passively encourage incompetence on many levels. Just such a long and all-too-familiar process came to a tipping point aboard the Waesche on November 11th, 2013, and one life needlessly ended while many others were permanently damaged.

* * *

NO MATTER WHAT FAMILY, ship, unit or group of friends Obie found himself in, his nature was to smile and make the best of it. People who knew him agree that he was positive and upbeat. He was always looking for the brightness in any gloom and was ready with kind words, bear hugs and encouragement for others. An example of Obie's selflessness can be seen in his approach to leave. On many occasions, especially those involving holidays, Obie would give up his leave so that a married shipmate could go and spend time with his or her family. This kindness always taxed me, as I was always eager to welcome him home, yet I was also very proud of him. My son's compassion and self-sacrifice never surprised me. Kindness filled his soul. It was how he lived.

Kindness made him happy. Love made him smile.

The meditation teacher and actor Jeff Kober ends one of his daily newsletters with these words: "Today I will choose to love someone for no other reason than because I can, and I will not ask for their permission, nor will I ask for anything in return." That pretty much describes how Obie loved; it's how he lived. He lived to love.

FOIA REQUEST

In January 2020, I submitted a written formal request to the United States Coast Guard under the Freedom of Information Act. I did so because I wanted all of the information that I felt had been suppressed in the formal investigation. I submitted my request via certified mail with return receipt requested and a signature required.

Weeks went by with me never receiving the return receipt confirming delivery nor any notification from the FOIA Department verifying that they had opened and assigned a case number. I finally traced it, and discovered that my request had indeed been delivered appropriately but that the Coast Guard had failed to acknowledge my request. Someone suggested I contact my Senator's office to seek their assistance, I reached out to them in February, submitting the paperwork they required, and the office then contacted USCG FOIA in early March. The Coast Guard responded to my Senator's office within a week in early March. My request had been assigned a case number, for which I was so grateful.

Eight days later I received a phone call from a staff attorney for the USCG. He explained that he worked with the FOIA office and was helping out during the general COVID-19 pandemic shutdown. The attorney asked me what specific information I wanted. He asked if I knew that a copy of the investigation results was available online. I explained that I had a copy of that report, but I also knew there was a lot more information that had been suppressed and I would like to see it.

I shared that Commandant Z told me that he would contact me with results from the MAB portion of the investigation, but I never heard from him or anyone in Command. All I wanted was the truth.

The attorney explained that the MAB result was not something for which I'd be granted access. It was a more in-depth investigation that MIGHT INCLUDE INFORMATION THAT COULD PROVE DAMAGING FOR SOME PEOPLE._The attorney went on to explain that there were timeframes for holding investigation information; he thought I already had everything that was available, but that he would check to make sure. The following day, he called to assure me that, yes, I had in fact, received all of the information to which I was entitled. He then asked if there was anything more that he could do for me. He added that, if it helped me at all, *I SHOULD KNOW THAT MY SON CONTINUED TO SAVE LIVES SINCE, THE DAY HE DIED BECAUSE OF THE CHANGES THAT HAVE BEEN IMPLEMENTED.* He also thanked me for his sacrifice and service. I thanked him and replied that I had been told that by many others and that I was grateful that no one else had to die, but I wish it had not taken my son's death for these changes to be made. Why weren't they made four years prior? Of course, there was no response to my statement, what could be said? I had already been told it wasn't a priority.

After our conversation, I waited for a formal letter confirming that my case request had been fulfilled and my file closed. I assumed that the letter would reach me via my Senator's office. Instead, I received a call from that office asking if I had gotten in touch with the contact person assigned to my case. I responded no, then explained what had transpired with the USCG attorney. The woman I spoke to in my Senator's office said it all sounded rather odd and that she was going to contact them directly. It was the second week of July that I received an email from my Senator's office with documents attached from USCG FOIA. The letter stated their decision on what was released and indicated that I could appeal the decision if I chose to do so. I thought about it and almost did appeal, yet I realized that I would not be any farther ahead than I was at that time. I knew I would not receive more information from the USCG regarding the death of my son. They couldn't or wouldn't release more information because it could be damaging and it was always apparent that the USCG was protecting its chain of command.

In the FOIA report, they even made obvious, careless mistakes. The name of the fishing vessel, for instance, wasn't even correct, it was referred to as the ARTIC MIST rather than the ALASKA MIST. It seemed like another example of how little the life of my son meant to them, or at least to those preparing the FOIA report. How little the Coast Guard cared about the death of a low-ranking Coastie. Their priority was clear. Focus on how best to protect and uphold the reputation of the United States Coast Guard and those in Command to the public eye.

What follows is the official letter to me that accompanied portions of the final report from the investigation into the death of my son, Obie. Reading it over, as I have many times, I wonder why transparency is being denied. Why the need for so much secrecy? What is the Coast Guard Command hiding? I deserve to know. The parents and loved ones of every Coastie deserves to know. Those that were on the ship that day deserve to know and all those that serve in the Coast Guard have the right to know. Until the truth is told, all we can do is continue to ask for it.

Commandant
United States Coast Guard

2703 Martin Luther King Jr Ave, SE
Washington, DC 20593-7907
Staff Symbol: CG-1131
Phone: (202) 475-4162

5720
FOIA: 2020-CGFO-0090'
05 JUNE 2020

Laurie Powell

Dear Mrs. Powell,

This is a response to your Freedom of Information Act (FOIA) request to the U.S. Coast Guard
(USCG), dated January 21, 2020 and received by this office on May 8, 2020. A copy of the
Major Incident Investigation (MII) with exhibits for the Coast Guard Cutter Waesche mishap
that occurred on November 11, 2013 was previously provided to you by Coast Guard Pacific
Area. We have been informed that you are seeking a copy of the full Mishap Analysis Report
(MAR) with attachments for the same mishap.

A search of Coast Guard Safety Division (CG-1131) records for documents responsive to your
request produced a total of 49 pages. Of those pages, I have determined that 4 pages of the
records are releasable in their entirety, 6 pages are partially releasable, and 39 pages are withheld
in their entirety pursuant to 5 U.S.C. § 552(b)(5), (b)(6) and (b)(7).

Aside from the four pages herein release in their entirety, enclosed as well are 6 pages of the
MAR with certain information withheld, as described below:

Personal information in the MAR is being withheld under 5 U.S.C. § 552(b))(6) because there
are clearly identifiable privacy interests in this information and release of this material would
likely cause particular harm to those privacy interests. I have considered the general public
interest in releasing this information, but in each case where I recommend withholding
information under FOIA Exemption (b)(6), the balance clearly tilts in favor of protecting the
privacy interest of individuals rather than any general public interest in release.

As mention, there are 39 pages of the MAR withheld, as described below:

The intra-agency information in the MAR is being withheld under 5 U.S.C. § 552(b)(5) because
it contains agency deliberations that do not reflect the final agency decision and disclosure would
discourage open and frank discussions in future deliberations and would cause public confusion
resulting from disclosure of reasons that were not ultimately the grounds for the agency's action.

Additionally, deliberative process information in the MAR is being withheld under 5 U.S.C.
552(b)(7) because deliberative process privilege protects the integrity of the deliberative or
decision-making processes within the agency by exempting from mandatory disclosure opinions,

conclusions, and recommendations included within inter-agency or intra-agency memoranda or letters. Each witness interviewed by the Mishap Analysis Board was read a statement of privilege. The release of this internal information would discourage the expression of candid opinions and inhibit the free and frank exchange of information among agency personnel. The condition of confidentiality was stamped on the report and accepted by the investigator with that condition. Release of this information could prevent the Coast Guard from receiving this type of information for use in future investigations.

I am the person responsible for the partial denial of your request. Also participating in this decision are Commander Jeremy Denning, Chief, Safety Division, and Commander Angel Galinanes, Office of Information and Intelligence Law.

You have a right to appeal the above-withholding determination. Should you wish to do so, you must send your appeal and a copy of this letter, within 60 days of the date of this letter, to:

> COMMANDANT (CG-6P)
> US COAST GUARD
> ATTN: FOIA/PA OFFICER
> 2703 MARTIN LUTHER KING JR AVE STOP 7101
> WASHINGTON DC 20593-7101

Following the procedures outlined in the DHS regulations at 6 C.F.R. § 5.9, your envelope and letter should be marked "FOIA Appeal." Copies of the FOIA and DHS regulations are available at www.dhs.gov/foia.

Provisions of the FOIA AND PRIVACY ACT allow us to recover part of the cost of complying with your request. In this instance, because the cost is below the $14 minimum, there is no charge. 6 CFR § 5.11(d)(4).

If you need to contact our office again about this matter, please refer to **2020-CGFO-00907**. This office can be reached at (202) 475-5162.

I hope this information satisfies your request. Should you need further assistance, or if you would like to discuss any aspect of your request, please contact Mr. Glenn L. Gebele, Chief, Office of Safety and Environmental Health. He can be reached at (202) 475-5195. Please refer to FOIA **2010-CGFO-00907** in your correspondence.

Sincerely,

DANA L. THOMAS
Rear Admiral, U.S. Coast Guard
Director, Health, Safety and Work-Life

I am torn trying to decide whether or not I should appeal the Coast Guard's determination. I understand the importance of protecting people that serve, yet my son was not afforded that level of protection.

In many ways, I love and support the grand mission of the U.S. Coast Guard. I want so much to believe that all of the people involved in the investigation did their best. Yet, I keep coming back to the fact that 39 out of 49 pages of details have been restricted and refused to me. Why? What does the bulk of the investigative report actually say? As the surviving mother of my only son, do I not have the right to know more? Why was this reckless decision made? Who was to benefit?

I feel very strongly that I do have that right and I should be able to see it. My son purchased the right for me to see it with his own life, a young life sacrificed in the line of duty.

EMAILS FROM THE DAY OF THE INCIDENT

The following emails were released by the Coast Guard and they paint a useful picture of the communications that took place between the decision makers of this evolution. Please note the non-urgent nature of fishing vessel's situation, the determined mindset of the Captain of the Waesche, the options that all parties had to stop this evolution from transpiring. Why were helicopters not used, when the small boat was sent in to operate beyond sea-condition regulations? Why was the throw line not used? And, could this really be the full log of communications between Commanders and coordinators given the extent of this "urgent" and "life threatening" SAR event? Why would some of these messages be redacted? What could possibly be classified in this case? Each reader must decide.

EMAIL 11/11/13 0711: CHIEF OF INCIDENT MANAGEMENT TO WAESCHE
"I apologize to you and your crew for diverting WAESCHE just prior to your MPB, but I need a federal response now that commercial has totally messed things up. ALASKA MIST is anchored and holding. Sister ship, F/V PAVLOF, is enroute to stand by to assist with 0930L ETA. Tug RESOLVE has one fouled screw and is standing by with intent to return to DH (Dutch Harbor) on non-folded screw. Working on

identifying non-essential personnel on ALASKA MIST for possible removal by helicopters. H60 in CB (Cold Bay) is ready to respond as necessary. Intend to reposition H65 to CB (Cold Bay) for response as necessary. Need WAESCHE to assume tow if able. Will keep you posted. Thanks!"

EMAIL 0725: WAESCHE/CAPTAIN TO CHIEF OF INCIDENT MANAGEMENT

"No problem on divert - that's why we're here. We're headed enroute now and anticipate an ETA about 1600. We'll try to establish direct comms with vessel this morning to get a better understanding of their ground tackle/configuration up forward and best means to rig a tow when we arrive later today."

EMAIL 0900: CHIEF OF INCIDENT MANAGEMENT TO WAESCHE

"F/V ALASKA Mist anchored and holding 8.5 NM (nautical miles) from the closest point of land. F/V PAVLOF enroute with 0930L ETA. Intent of PAVLOF is O/S (on scene) presence in case anchor doesn't hold. RESOLVE coordinating to have helicopter with diver o/s (on scene) to un-foul screw with midday ETR. WAESCHE's H65 being repositioned from D/H (Dutch Harbor) to CB (Cold Bay). CB (Cold Bay) H60 on alert and is approximately 30 NM from distress scene. F/V ALASKA MIST identifying non-essential personnel, but plan to leave on ship unless situation worsens. Weather forecast to improve throughout the day and remainder of the week (see attached email). Plan is to have WAESCHE assume TOW, but may reconsider using RESOLVE if they get repaired and can assume tow without worsening the situation. Either way, desire WAESCHE to continue to distress scene given my apprehension with RESOLVE capability. Would greatly appreciate you establishing direct comms with ALASKA MIST as soon as able. Still haven't heard back via my watch, but is WAESCHE capable of assuming TOW given ALASKA MIST's tonnage and taking vessel to DH?"

EMAIL 0920: WAESCHE/CAPTAIN TO CHIEF OF INCIDENT MANAGEMENT

"We are capable of taking them in tow. We are attempting to call the ALASKA MIST directly to obtain some additional details from planning. We are going to push to get there before 1600; we just came up on turbine and will run as fast as the seas/swells allow. Will update ETA with CC (Command Center) as we adjust our timeline. Once onscene and wx (weather) permitting, we will put a few of our folks onboard via our small boat to assist in rigging the tow. We can remove any unnecessary personnel from the F/V at that time if desired. I'd rather do that icw taking them in tow vice later at night if condition/situation changes."

EMAIL 1011: CHIEF OF INCIDENT MANAGEMENT TO WAESCHE

"Sounds great and definitely glad we've got WAESCHE responding. Know my CC watch passed ALASKA MIST iridium number to WAESCHE, but let us know if you need anything else to help establish direct comms between WAESCHE and ALASKA MIST. Concur on your plan to put folks onboard ALASKA MIST once o/s. Would like you to plan to remove all non-essential personnel before night fall (sunset is 1752L) via small boat if able just in case condition/situation worsens. H60/H65 will remain on stand-by in CB to assist with removing non-essential personnel if needed or to respond sooner if situation worsens before WAESCHE arrives o/s. Current status: PAVLOF is o/s standing by. 6544 should be airborne shortly enr (enroute) CB (Cold Bay) with approximate one-hour flight time. RESOLVE repair has been delayed until late afternoon arrival of their helo (~1700L ETA) with expected ETR later this evening. Will plan for WAESCHE as primary towing option with RESOLVE as back-up option."

EMAIL 1017: ~~REDACTED~~ TO D17 DISTRICT COMMAND CENTER
"We have been unable to reach the ALASKA MIST using the IRIDIUM phone number passed. Could you reach out to them and obtain answers to the attached list of questions and send back to us?"

EMAIL 1129: WAESCHE TO INCIDENT MANAGEMENT
"Sounds good - we've increased speed and should arrive ooa 1430. We will access on-scene conditions and plan to disembark non-essential personnel icw putting a few of our folks onboard if we're in parameters for small boat ops. We're going to go through our towing brief before we arrive and then reassess conditions once we arrive to determine best way to get our messenger over. Using small boat would be my preference since they're anchored and that limits our ability to maneuver around them. Our CIC watch will keep the CC posted with updates once we arrive on scene."

EMAIL 1132: D17 TO WAESCHE
"Here is the attached reply to the form sent to the vessel. I will follow up with an email detailing non-essential personnel on board."

EMAIL 1151: ~~REDACTED~~

EMAIL 1159: BRANCH MANAGEMENT TO WAESCHE/CAPTAIN
"Just got out of my CC and got the brief on comms issues. May just be the course you're on now. Email appears to be the most reliable method of communicating between all assets as CC has just gotten email back from ALASKA MIST as well. Know they pushed ALASKA MIST email to you, so recommend you have your OPS try to reach out via email, so you can start to get better assessment of ALASKA MIST ground/tackle configuration. Will try to connect via voice once you've conducted o/s assessment and have recommended COA. Will be just you and me discussing COA, and then I'll back the brief COS/DR. Couple of things to have in your back pocket for planning. State of

Alaska has an Emergency Towing System (ETS) small (<50,000 DWT) in CB, which has the ability to be deployed to your vessel via H60 sling ops if needed in an emergency. Here's the weblink to get more info: dec.alaska.gov./SPAR/perp/ets/. There is an ETS large (<50,000 DWT) at AS Kodiak that I can get moved to CB via C130 if need be. Whatever COA we decide, would prefer to have ALASKA MIST recover anchor if able, so we don't lose the option to use it again if necessary. Thanks for coming up on turbines, as 1430L ETA is very much appreciated."

EMAIL 1231: ALASKA MIST/MASTER TO ~~REDACTED~~

"I've decided to keep a total of 8 essential crew members on board. It is my understanding that the Coast Guard Cutter #751 will be transiting non-essential crew to their vessel."

EMAIL 1300: WAESCHE TO INCIDENT BRANCH

"Roger-we're about 30NM from ALASKA MIST position now so should be getting within VHF range soon and will brief them on our plan so they can begin to identify personnel for transfer. I will be on the bridge during this entire evolution so will relay our COA via WAE OPS using HLS Net to D17 CC to brief you. We'll be managing the daylight we have so I'd appreciate a quick turn-around on concur/non-concur on our plan when we provide it. Concur with trying to keep the anchor, but will need to see if that is going to impact our ability to rig the tow and make assessment. We'll be in touch in the coming hours...headed to tow brief now."

EMAIL 1301: WAESCHE/CAPTAIN TO WAESCHE/OPS

"OPS-wrt below, I'll need you to be our "comms relay" to DRM on our plan from CIC once we determine our COA. I've asked for quick concurrence so hopefully, we'll get that after they brief it up."

EMAIL 1303: ALASKA MIST TO ~~REDACTED~~
~~Redacted~~

EMAIL 1303: ALASKA MIST TO WAESCHE/OPS

"We are always on standby on 4125 with 2 separate MFHF radios though if you choose a frequency for coms we will shift one radio over to that frequency gladly. Our vessel has sharp bow with very slight rake. There is not bulbous bow. We have two mooring chaulks 8ft aft of the tip of the bow on the port and starboard side. We have two 10-inch x 30 inch double bits located 20 feet aft of the tip of the bow on the port and starboard side. The Foxhole section of this vessel is an ex-military Yard Oiler- The forward structure is very heavily framed. These bits were used to tow this vessel from Dutch Harbor to Seattle Via ocean-going tug in approx 2005 for an engine replacement and they are very secure. Also, I forwarded our last email concerning essential crew-keeping total of 8 persons on board. Though we are only equipped with survival suits as required for each individual on this vessel. It is my experience that the survival suits do not offer much in the way of dexterity climbing up or down a pilot ladder."

EMAIL 1307: ALASKA MIST TO WAESCHE OPS

"Our Sat phone is operational and we can also call you if you have a phone number we can reach you at. I believe I sent both numbers in my first reply to your questions also. Email here is only On demand iridium. We have to log on to our server to see if an email has been sent to us. Your support and aid in assisting us is very much appreciated."

EMAIL 1315: INCIDENT MANAGEMENT TO WAESCHE/CAPTAIN

"Sounds great. Completely trust your judgement and will respond quickly to recommend COA. FYI, ALASKA MIST has already identified 14 non-essential personnel with eight essential personnel remaining onboard. Concur on anchor thought process. Standing by.

Thanks."

COLLECTION OF MEMORIES

I've included these memories from my son's shipmates and friends because they are heartfelt and help me tell a larger story about my son and the person he was, his character. I am grateful to all of those that shared.

Letter from a shipmate/friend:

"It's difficult to express in words how amazing it was to meet you two along with your family and friends. The amount of love that was shared was immeasurable.

"Travis was so amazing. He was my boss he came to the *Waesche*. The morale and overall crew attitude was probably as low as it could have been when he reported. Personally, I was spiraling down into a depression that came slowly over time from being in a negative environment I couldn't get out of. Travis seemed to turn it all around once he came to the *Waesche*.

"It didn't take long for Travis' smiling face to turn around our department's attitude. He could walk into a room and the entire atmosphere would change. It was like his positive energy transferred to everyone he interacted with. It was like the 'happiness flu'; super contagious and everyone got it (ha ha).

It didn't matter what ridiculous task we were assigned. Travis would throw a positive spin on it and before we knew it, we were done; laughing and smiling the whole time.

"Travis was the breath of fresh air everyone needed. He had an amazing soul and as I sit here and write, I realize that I have actually carried some of that positive energy with me. He touched lives and after meeting the people he grew up around, it makes sense; he came from a family of amazing people."

These are memories from Obie's dear friend from Boston:

Here are just a few of the memories I have with Travis. I will send you some more. I am beyond grateful for the Good Lord allowing me to have him as a brother and part of my journey through life.

First Meeting:

I first met Obie when I was assigned to Station Boston in 2010. I remember one of the first time we did a project/ task together. We were told to do some work on the sliding window/ door on one of the 25' RBS boats that was tied up to the pier. Of course the door we had to work on was on the water side and not one that was accessible from the pier. So, being the one that wanted to get the job done without haste, I made my way around the outside of the boat and began to work. Well, trying to work with one hand hold myself to the boat and my other hand, it became evident that the potential to lose my grip and take a swim in the water was a good possibility. Thankfully Obie was a clear thinker and realized the situation i had put myself in. He made a suggestion, but looking back on it now was more of a polite way of calling me a dumbass, that I should put on a life jacket and tether myself to the boat by using a harness type line thus leaving both of my hands free and greatly reducing the chance of me taking the plunge. It was at this moment that I knew he was one to always look out for his shipmates and was sometimes the voice of reason. We completed out work without incident and carried on with our day.

Standing Duty:

Obie and I became good friends and eventually developed a brother like relationship. After knowing each other for some time, living in the same berthing room, and being rack mates, I would always greet him every morning with a loud "Good morning Obie!!" and immediately give him a big tight hug. He would crack a half ass smile most of the time and as we shared our morning greeting I would always tell him that i loved him. He would always respond "I love you too."

Obie and I shared many similar experiences at the station. When we were going for our coxswain qualification, we went through the same trials and failures. Both of us spent lots of time, some of it was even our off days, working on becoming qualified to drive the units small boats. Although often feeling defeated, angry, tired, and when we thought there was no end in sight, we knew we were both going through the same thing. It was having him with me that helped progress through these difficult times. I was with him on his check rides always trying to help in any way i could and pushing him to keep going.

Obie had a personality about him not seen in many people these days. He had a gift of compassion, understanding, the ability to listen and mentor in times that if it was me in those situations I would have walked away. But not Obie. He was a rockstar!

As days, weeks, months and years went buy we continued to share the best and worst times together. All of us in the duty section had a soft spot for the "Muscle Hamster" as we referred to him. I couldn't be more proud to have known and served with him.

Joking around:

As is with all units, morale is a life saver! And who better to play jokes on or set some one else up for a joke than Obie. I quickly became aware of how much he loved reading what most referred to as "wizard books." Before most would even think of hitting the rack for the night, Obie was tucked into his rack with his makeshift curtains tucked beneath my mattress (I had the rack above his) and he would be quietly reading. I would sometime blast into the room, rip open his curtain, and exclaim "Hey Buddy!!" This was more often than not quickly followed but some choice words from him, an angry glance, and then a hand pulling his curtain closed.

Another thing that was a big mistake to joke about was when he was engaged in a video game. This became more than apparent when I thought it would be a good idea to shut his game off when he was in the middle of playing. It was weekend duty and Obie was playing a game on the Rec Deck. This was the common room in which all personnel could watch a program, sporting event, or movie on the big TV. Well, I decided that wanting to watch something other than Obie play his game was more important. Instead of doing the polite and correct action of asking him to pause or finish his game, I made the terrible decision of shutting it off by pushing the power button. Big mistake!!! The Muscle Hamster stood up, gave me a death glare that could have conquered Gangas Kahn himself, grabbed the Xbox and stormed off without saying a word. He went into our room and disappeared for a few hours. Not knowing if i had just signed my own death warrant and being told by others who had just witnessed this dastardly event take place that I was crazy for doing that, I hesitantly and cautiously made my way into the berthing room to apologize. Cautiously and slowly I walked into the berthing room and made my way over to where he was sitting on the couch. I told him I was truly sorry and gave him a huge long hug. A slight smile came across his face and I knew I would live to see another day. I told him I would never do that again and that I loved him. Once again in true Obie style he told me he loved me but not to ever mess with him while he was playing video games.

As I sit here typing out some of the memories, I am overcome with all types of emotions. Typing through tears, laughs, but most importantly remembering the times I was allowed to share and spend with him really puts into prospective of how much you can bond with someone that you never thought you would ever meet. I only spent 3 years with him, but it only took 3 minutes to call him my brother. I love you bro...

I will send you some more memories this weekend!

I love you!!

-B

Memories from a CG Supervisor

I had the privilege of serving with Travis (Obie) onboard Waesche, while I was a LTJG on my second tour afloat. Travis was on my boarding team: one of the best and most reliable members! Over the course of our Alaska Patrol, we did dozens of boardings together. Having him on my team made it a really enjoyable experience. Although I'd always been interested in the fisheries, it was actually him that I first spoke with about the possibility of going to grad school and shifting my career to fisheries full time. His encouragement stuck with me so much that after we returned to port, in late November, I signed up to take the GRE. About 6 months before my required 5 years of service came up, I finally got the guts to apply for grad school. I was accepted, left the service in 2016 and completed my masters degree in Marine Affairs in 2017. I have been working full time in fisheries policy (with the fishing community) for the past 3 years. Although there have been many moments of sadness as I look back on my time in Alaska and on Waesche, I'm equally as grateful for the time that I did spend in Travis' company, because it changed my entire career and life. Thank you so much for the opportunity to share our memories, and I wish you and your family all the best this holiday season.

Friend and Shipmate

Him and I had decided we were tired of hanging out in the bar and decided to go ahead of everyone else and prep a big bon fire on the beach/shore in Dutch Harbor. By this point though the group had done so many bonfires that firewood was becoming more scarce. I remember him and I branched off to search for more. I came back feeling pretty good about myself carrying a few heavy pieces. All of a sudden I see him carrying a telephone pole down the beach. I couldn't even help I was too busy laughing.

Another memory:

I just needed to share this with you while it's still fresh in my mind. JT had on one of Trav's Memorial shirts the other day, he is in NC training. A young man approached him and said he knew Obie, that he worked for him in Boston. So...JT called me and asked if I would like to speak with him, of course I did...

He of course offered his condolences and then told me what an amazing person Obie was, that he learned a lot from him while working for him. He said the one thing that he so admired about him and he has taken it with him in his leadership was....they would address him as Petty Officer Obendorf and he would say, please don't call me that, either call me Obie or Travis. Because even though I out rank you, we are all equal.....

No one was ever below him, everyone was equal.....

From another friend/shipmate:

Have you ever asked yourself why? Why do the nicest people on this planet go first? I have. I've always wondered why GOD would take such a pure soul. I've finally came to a conclusion. GOD needs all the Angels he can get, to watch out for the rest of us. This may be my way of coping, but I find it peaceful.

When GOD took one of his angels, he took one of the few pure souls I will ever have the pleasure knowing. His name, Travis Obendorf (OB).

I remember the first time I met OB. It was in the Coast Guard. He reported to my unit, and I remember thinking he was huge. He immediately earned the name The Hulk. He was the biggest male on board, yet wore the tightest of the tightest of shirts. From my understanding, no one on board had a negative thing to say about him. He was a hard worker, very personable, and hilarious. Most of all he was passionate. Hard core "Joe Coastie."

How we began our friendship was, he was my boss. He was in charge of about 8 of us. Most of the time, he would task us, then join in and help. This was rare on board so it was noticed. Higher ups, enjoyed him, us lower folks enjoyed him. He was much loved. We stood watch together. I was a lookout, I would stand on the bridge wings and look out, and take over the helm if needed. Travis was the BMOW, which is comparable to "security" of a ship. He would make rounds of the ship to make sure everything was working properly. We had watch together often. He use to make me coffee. Since most times it was freezing outside, it would help warm me up. He never would tell me what he would put in it, and it was the best damn coffee I've ever had. I must have asked him over 100 times how he made it, and he said he would have to kill me first if he told.

One day in the P-way "hallways" of the ship, we were supposed to be doing sweepers, which is what it sounds like, sweeping the decks of the ship, and he jumped on my back and said "carry me!" I did mention he was the biggest male on board, so I of course collapsed. I told him that was an unfair shot, so I tried again. I've never carried that much weight, but I made it 5 steps till my legs gave out.

These memories seem little and trivial, but they were everything to me. Especially now since that's all I have of him.

I remember the day of his incident so well. It was the worst weather. We had a navy weather specialist on board to help guide us. We had received a call that a vessel in the bearing sea needed assistance. They were DIW (dead in the water) their engines had stopped, so they needed a tow. They had a person on board that was injured already so they didn't want to risk it. As the Coast Guard that's what we do, so we make way to the vessel "Alaska Mist." (I'll never forget that vessel name). We finally end up near the Alaska Mist and we have done our Risk Assessments, and its time to launch the small boat off our stern so we could recover the personnel on board their ship, and transport them to ours for safety. It's the bearing sea, so it's pretty bad weather. I am part of deck crew, so I am part of the operation of launching the boat and I had the task to launch the life ring when necessary, and another member on deck had the task to hold the winch line, which is what hauls the small boat back into the stern of the ship. Their job was to pull it to release, and when the small boat returns they send it over to whichever crew member sits on the bow of the small boat to attach, so our winch can haul the small boat back up. So operations go normal releasing the small boat out into the water, and there are 2 crew members conducting the same position, Travis and another crew member. They have to decide who wants to stay on board the Alaska Mist while the small boat and the rest of the crew transport the civilians. They finally come to a decision of the other crew member to stay on the Alaska Mist, while Travis goes back onto the small boat to transport their crew members off the vessel onto our Coast Guard Cutter. The seas have heightened by this point, but operations remain looking safe, as safe as they can in these seas. Time for the small boat to return into the cutters stern, and it got bad.

The seas were pushing the small boat all over the place and the coxswain was doing his best to maintain course. The coxswain gets it semi lined up to winch up into the stern of the cutter and the waves were so strong it pushed the small boat up too fast. The deck crew member throws over the winch line and Travis doesn't have a chance to connect it, and as everyone starts to worry, a huge wave pushes the small boat up insanely too far into the stern, causing the winch net to go over the small boat bow and crush Travis between the net and the small boat console. The wave backed off, and the small boat went down slowly with the wave. Everyone on deck was worried and nervous if everyone was ok. So we are yelling, holding up the thumbs up to see if Travis responds, and he does. He held a thumbs up back to us, looking a little impaired, but seems to be ok. As he is gaining his balance back the wave comes back, bigger, and stronger and pushes the small boat back up into the stern of the cutter. Again, and again, and again.

At this point we all know Travis is not ok. We see a lot of blood, and Travis is unconscious. Everyone, including the coxswain is doing everything they can to help get him out of the boat to safety. As I stated before, the waves were coming in so strong, so this was a hard task for them. They get him off the boat, rip off his dry suit the best they can and take off all his head gear, and try to assess his injuries. He is bleeding, and unconscious. Our ships medical team gathers on the deck and transports him to the mess deck which is a make shift operating table with all the medical supplies our ship could utilize. They administer CPR while we wait for a rescue helicopter to transport him off the cutter and to a hospital. During this time, I cannot be a part of this since I am not on the medical team. I am a wreck. Anyone who was there was a wreck, but we have civilian personnel we still need to take care of. The people in charge of this operation were all a wreck as well, but we had a responsibility to complete this towing evolution. We gathered to address what had just happened and to talk about how we still have a duty to fulfill, so we start back up on the evolution. I will not be lying when I say that this was one of the hardest things I had to do. Everyone has a different story, a different background, but for me, this was hard. I took it very poorly. Thankfully we had a supportive chain of command who brought a chaplain on board to allow us the opportunity to talk it out, which none of us did. I was at least thankful and appreciative of that opportunity knowing that if I needed to talk that I could. Not just with the chaplain but anyone on board. I was grateful for my friends, who helped me get through that time. Witnessing something so traumatizing is one thing, knowing who the victim is, and having a connection with them, makes it a whole new story.

Knowing that a good friend of mine was hurt made it that much more difficult to continue the rest of the ALPAT patrol in the bearing sea. The only thing making it any easier was receiving updates about how he was doing in the hospital, and knowing other Coast Guard members in Seattle were visiting him and making him feel loved. His family had to endure a hard thing during the few last months of his life, seeing someone they loved and cherished, hurt. They are so strong for that, and I hope they felt the love as well from all of us that reached out.

I am forever grateful and truly blessed to have met Travis Obendorf. I will never forget him and our beautiful friendship. I miss him dearly, and I know he is my guardian angel. He was truly an amazing person. <3 Every time I hear the song California Love <3 R.I.P OB <3

PHONE CONVERSATIONS – TRANSCRIPTS

These are various quotes received from many of Obie's shipmates/friends. They all had the same things to say:

"The captain and upper command of the CG were trying to save face after everything happened, that's why they tried to keep it all so quiet and blamed the crew.

"The National Security Cutters were newest, latest and greatest in the CG and they just wanted to prove what they could do and didn't care about the crew. Ego took over and they lost track of the mission."

"We were human beings first and they forgot that! We were just numbers."

"The command was toxic."

"The Captain wouldn't even interact with them. He acted like he was above them. He made it obvious that he didn't care about his crew."

"One of the worst things was the ships next to us (Stratton & Bertholf). They all had signs up and were doing things to honor OBIE and we couldn't even talk about him. We weren't allowed to do anything for him. The things we tried to do, we were ordered to take down or couldn't wear."

"The whole command at that time had lost track of what the Coast Guard stands for."

These are words from a retired CG Captain:

"Unless the F/V was on fire, at risk of sinking or capsizing, you just don't put your crew at the risk that they did. As long as they had power there was no reason that they could not have stood by and waited until the conditions improved."

Words from another young shipmate/friend from the ship:

"The captain was after and Admirals Star.

"The command had been hoping to get on *The Deadliest Catch*.

"The small rescue craft that was on the ship and used on that day wasn't even rated for those waters; not in regulations."

The Coxswains had told him that he had felt pressured into doing the mission by the command. After the incident, they put the totaled SRP (small rescue craft) in the yard and didn't even have the decency to cover it up. He said that they all had to walk past it, day in and day out and look at it. It was horrible!

"What holds together the tradition of command is inescapable accountability. How many times do we hear people say they take full responsibility for some disaster, and then nothing happens to them? No Accountability. Without accountability there can be no trust from your crew, especially in times of danger. If they don't trust you, you're finished." – US Navy Commanding Officer, Peter Squicciarini (Ret.)

FOR OUR CHILDREN

We are left behind, but not alone
We struggle to face each and every new day
But we do it, For Our Children

Sometimes the darkness and emptiness is more than we can bear
A darkness and emptiness that only a mother can know
But, we try to find the light, For Our children

We put on our shoes each day as if they were "Their" boots
We put a brave face on each day, just as they did
We trudge forward each day, For Our Children

They made us so proud, from the day that they were born
And continue to do so in the days after they are gone
They are Our Children

They have made the ultimate sacrafice
They have given their All, for All
They Were Our Children

For Them, and because of Them we carry on
Because of Them, and in honor of Them
We do it All, For Our Children

Written by Laurie Powell
In Loving Memory of BM3 Travis R. Obendorf ~ My Beautiful Son

Made in the USA
Las Vegas, NV
29 July 2021